TURNAROUND AND BEYOND

More Praise for *Turnaround and Beyond*

"Crandall's *Turnaround and Beyond* is easy to read, insightful, packed with helpful suggestions, and strategic in revitalizing stagnant and declining small churches that were once full of vigor and vitality. This is an indispensable book for anyone who believes that God wills his church to grow."
—Tetsunao Yamamori, Senior Fellow, Center for Religion and Civic Culture, University of Southern California

"Rural setting or not, smaller church or not; if you are concerned about renewal and revitalization, read and reread *Turnaround and Beyond*. It is an expansive yet concise guide to proven strategies and an introduction to a promising new development that could launch a renewal movement."
—Alan Rice, Director of Rural Ministry and Community Development, Western North Carolina Conference of The United Methodist Church

"Church members as well as pastors, looking for a new and fresh day in the life of their smaller-membership congregation, will surely come alive to a new vision and a new hope as they read this book! Not only does Ron Crandall show you small-membership churches that are alive and vital, he shows you how it can happen in your church. In this book, you will find a reservoir of helpful material that links you to some of the greatest thinkers and practitioners of our day. I would like to think that all of my small-membership pastors were using this as a reference book as they lead their congregations into a meaningful and healthy future."
—Alfred W. Gwinn Jr., Resident Bishop, Raleigh Area, The United Methodist Church

". . . written with refreshing clarity based upon solid data-giving practical advice and tested direction to laity and clergy leaders who realize that small-membership churches can be precious jewels of faith development. [Ron Crandall] gives hope that these communities of faith can not only survive but also thrive in leading followers of Jesus in faithful mission and ministry."
—Jeffrey E. Greenway, Lead Pastor of the Reynoldsburg United Methodist Church near Columbus, Ohio

"Many long for the revitalization of small mainline Christian churches but don't know what to do or how to do it. Ron Crandall has laid out a plan that is based on empirical evidence and inspired by the Spirit. Not surprisingly, at the center is leadership development. Finding, cultivating, and supporting clergy and laypersons committed to small-membership churches is key. Many forces discourage the revitalization of small-membership churches, but Ron has helped to identify those forces and to develop strategies to overcome them. May all small-membership churches benefit from this fine work."
—Jack Ewing, Executive Director and CEO, The Foundation for Evangelism affiliated with The United Methodist Church

Turnaround and Beyond

A Hopeful Future for the Small Membership Church

Ron Crandall

Abingdon Press
Nashville

TURNAROUND AND BEYOND
A HOPEFUL FUTURE FOR THE SMALL MEMBERSHIP CHURCH

Copyright © 1995, 2008 by Abingdon Press

All rights reserved.

This book is printed on acid-free paper.

Library of Congress Cataloging-in-Publication Data

Crandall, Ronald K.
   Turnaround and beyond : a hopeful future for the small membership church / Ron Crandall.
      p.   cm.
   Rev. ed. of: Turnaround strategies for the small church. c1995.
   Includes bibliographical references and index.
   ISBN 978-0-687-64699-9 (binding: pkb., adhesive-perfect : alk. paper)
   1. Small churches.   I. Crandall, Ronald K. Turnaround strategies for the small church.   II. Title.

BV637.8.C73   2008
254—dc22

                                                                    2008031809

08 09 10 11 12 13 14 15 16 17—10 9 8 7 6 5 4 3 2 1

MANUFACTURED IN THE UNITED STATES OF AMERICA

Contents

Acknowledgments

Looking back on our lives, which of us could ever have imagined the impact that certain people or unexpected events would have on our life stories?

I did not grow up in the church. When I was nine, a friend risked asking me tough questions before I realized there was a dimension of life I had not yet explored. My sister, as a teenager, had to follow a divine nudge and go to church alone on Sunday mornings searching for answers. Neighbors had to reach out to my parents and invite us all to go with them before we made it to church as a family and were baptized. Each of these persons and countless others who probably never knew the impact they would have are those to whom I owe a great debt.

I almost stumbled into my deep appreciation and concern for smaller churches. When I was a senior in college, my pastor asked me if I could preach. I wondered why he would ask such a strange question. He told me a little mission church they supported needed someone to fill in for four weeks. I agreed to give it a try. Wheatfield Methodist Church averaged twelve persons in worship—my first experience in a "small church." I stayed for six months. I was probably not very helpful to them, but they loved me and expressed appreciation for my feeble efforts. At the end of those six months, I was on my way to seminary; and eight years later, after doctoral studies and serving on the staff in a larger church, I, along with my wife, Bonnie, and our one-year-old son, Matthew, was off to serve another small church near Phoenix, Arizona.

Neither of these seasons as the pastor of a smaller church was easy for me. I had a great deal to learn about myself and about loving and leading such congregations. Nevertheless, each of these experiences set me on a path that eventually led to who I am today and what I invest my life in as a friend and student of smaller congregations.

Smaller-membership churches are like families—for better and for worse. The most important element in any family is love. For all those who have invested their time and love to make this book possible, I am deeply grateful. Many of their names will be found in the appendix but the most important to me are those within my own family who love me and teach me. I'm grateful to Joshua, Matthew, Jennifer, Jordan, and Julia, and most of all to Bonnie, who has repeatedly sacrificed her time and plans to make me a better husband, father, pastor, teacher, and Christian.

Faith, hope, and love abide, but the greatest of these is love. It is the love of God and neighbor that best reveals the Spirit of God at work in us and enables every congregation of Christ's body, regardless of its size, to be fruitful and glorify God. May the stories, insights, strategies, and especially the love that permeates these pages be a gift to you and through you to others searching for their place in the family of amazing grace.

With gratitude for all those who have helped adopt me into the family,

Ron Crandall
June 2008

Preface

In 1995, when *Turnaround Strategies for the Small Church* was first researched and released, it described how smaller churches were *re*vitalized. To revitalize means to restore to a former vitality, or bring to new life. This kind of language revealed then, and still reveals, several of my assumptions.

First, I assume that smaller churches needing a *turnaround* must have once been strong and full of life—otherwise they could not be *re*vitalized, they would simply need to be *vitalized*.

Second, it seems clear that many such churches are suffering from some degree of self-doubt and are not experiencing or manifesting to the world all that they could of the life of Jesus Christ. They may or may not know the degree of their illness or how close they are to death, but survival has probably been a topic of conversation more than once. They realize they aren't what they used to be, and they usually have little sense of direction.

A third assumption is that all smaller churches are in some ways different from medium or larger churches, and therefore they deserve special study and their own prescriptions for renewed health. This is, of course, an assumption that has been ignored by many writers and teachers in the past; but most research today clearly establishes that this assumption is well founded and extremely important.

Fourth, I assume that smaller congregations that have declined over the years can be turned around. It is this assumption that gives thousands of faithful members and pastors of these churches hope during dark days of decay and decline. "It has happened before; it can happen again; it can happen to us" is an important realization.

A fifth assumption is that the real experts on small-church revitalization are the persons who have experienced it firsthand—the pastors and members of revitalized small churches.

By acting on this last assumption, the original *turnaround study* began with letters sent through the Net Results organization to key judicatory leaders in over fifty denominations, asking for nominations of smaller churches that had experienced a turnaround. The actual request read as follows:

> Would you identify for us two or three of your smaller churches (under 200 members and/or 100 at worship) which have shown a remarkable turnaround in the last two to five years, including: A new sense of hope and empowerment, a new vision for mission, a new readiness to reach out to the community, a new effectiveness in evangelism, and new growth in membership/church school/worship attendance?
>
> We are especially interested in looking at churches where the community context has not changed or at least cannot account for the experienced renewal and church growth.

Over 200 churches and pastors representing ten denominations were recommended by their judicatory leaders. Of these, 186 pastors could be contacted by letter and were asked to participate in the project by filling out a survey questionnaire. One hundred thirty-six agreed to participate and 97 returned the initial survey. Three additional pastors and their churches were selected by the author in order to produce one hundred stories of renewal in smaller congregations. It was this database and the wonderful insights and stories reported by both pastors and laypeople in these churches that informed *Turnaround Strategies for the Small Church.*

Turnaround and Beyond is an expanded revision of that original text and maintains the best insights from those one hundred stories of renewal as well as offering additional lessons gleaned from a more recent study of these same churches. Many of the comments made by those involved in the original study are maintained, but only a limited effort is made to link the information obtained from the more recent interviews with specific individuals, though I am deeply indebted to those who gave me their time and trust. Several of the outcomes of the follow-up study are examined in chapters 7 and 8, along with recommendations for maintaining the turnaround through the dangerous seasons of pastoral transitions.

A few months ago I met with new pastors serving in a district of The United Methodist Church. During the meeting the district superintendent stated that close to a third of the smaller congregations in the district would probably be closed within the next five to seven years. Denominational data all across the mainline spectrum, both here and abroad, and even in many of the more evangelical traditions in the West, indicate that this is not an isolated or unusual prediction. Of course, all small churches are not in such a desperate condition, no more than all large churches are healthy and growing. Nevertheless, many smaller churches are struggling, and every year thousands that were once vital congregations close their doors for the last time—some as mergers that have about a 50/50 chance of success, and others as churches writing the end of their story. Most of these congregations have been holding on, surviving, for years. But survival is not God's primary purpose for the church.

Almost every church that survives its first decade or two of existence has experienced vitality and growth through its outreach to persons coming to new faith in Christ. Churches are normally started with that goal in mind. A generation ago the generally accepted perception for sustained church growth was that after twenty-five to thirty years a church would plateau and begin to decline unless intentional new efforts were made to reach new people and grow. However, in this new century with its rapid acceleration of change and special new challenges of financial viability, that time line is shrinking. If a church isn't being "renewed" (some even say "reinvented") every ten years or so, its chances for continued health and impact on its community are severely limited.

As churches look backward to a former day of strength and vitality, they often begin to lose their sense of confidence in what God can do in them and through them in the present day and in the future. Overwhelmingly, smaller churches over fifty years old suffer from this malady. Many members of these churches and the pastors who serve them sometimes find it nearly impossible to "rejoice in the Lord always." But the testimonies of renewal reflected in the pages that follow are powerful messages of hope. Turnaround is happening, and there is a way for it to have an ongoing life, and not just be a short blip on the screen.

Do not remember the former things,
   or consider the things of old.
I am about to do a new thing;
   now it springs forth, do you not perceive it? . . .
for I give water in the wilderness,
   rivers in the desert,
to give drink to my chosen people,
   the people whom I formed for myself
so that they might declare my praise. (Isaiah 43:18-21)

CHAPTER 1
Pathways to Turnaround

*Turnaround: "A change of allegiance, opinion, mood,
or policy"*   *—Webster's Dictionary*

S ome of us are old enough to remember windup toys—batteries not included or needed. One of my favorites was a tin Jeep, which performed amazing feats. If wound and turned on by the flip of a small lever, it would whir and ding, spin around, lunge forward until it encountered some obstacle or precipice, automatically reverse itself, turn in a new direction, and move ahead once more. I found it wonderfully entertaining, and I worked hard to make the obstacles I placed in its path ever more challenging. Eventually, I succeeded in stalling the vehicle by boxing it in with just the right combination of restraints. Occasionally, at least in the mind of small boy, it even seemed to get frustrated, as it banged and bumped its way into a corner. Although it was designed with a built-in "turnaround mechanism," when it was cornered and immobilized, its energy source failed rapidly. The turning wheels slowed. The whirs and dings ceased. And as abruptly as it lunged forward with the flip of a switch, it stopped, dead.

It would be stretching things to say I looked at all this with any deep or morbid thoughts of life and death. After all, the rundown toy required only the hands of a small boy to free it and rewind it so it could start its wonderful dance all over again. But the image of that childhood toy, cornered and out of power, comes to mind as we begin to explore strategies that enable struggling and often rundown small churches to experience a turnaround, move forward again, and maintain their momentum for the glory of God.

Fifteen years ago, when I first began the research for *Turnaround Strategies for the Small Church,* very few organizations were using the language of "turnaround." Recently, however, when I typed "turnaround strategies" into my Web browser, 1,320,000 hits emerged, and multitudes of specialized consulting organizations promoted their skills. Although individual and corporate human problems require much more than a small boy's hands and the turn of a key, along the way persons do emerge who seem to know how to bring renewal to our lives and endeavors.

When the research for *Turnaround Strategies for the Small Church* began, one hundred pastors who had successfully employed turnaround strategies in their small churches emerged as such persons. Their formulas were not identical, but they had learned, one way or another, many of the same lessons. Frequently, they could not describe exactly what had happened that enabled their congregations to experience turnaround; but even without knowing it, they had utilized many of the same principles we now are able to describe as turnaround strategies.

Of course, since the church is not merely a human endeavor but the creation of God empowered by the Holy Spirit, few persons who have been involved in a genuine experience of turnaround in a local church would say the result is something they accomplished. But almost always, the work of the Spirit who brings new life to old and troubled churches is connected to the lives of men and women of faith who lead God's people to a new vision, a new hope, and a new identity.

Turnaround Theories

Because the experience of decline and immobility is not unique to smaller churches in our day, concerned persons of faith have always tried to warn against the dangers and offer hope to the distraught and defeated. It could be said that the primary function of the prophets was to call God's people to "re-turn" to their identity and their covenant as the children of God. God warned the Israelites through Moses: "take care that you do not forget the LORD, who brought you out of the land Egypt, out of the house of slavery. . . . Remember what the LORD your God did" (Deuteronomy 6:12; 7:18). Paul instructs the early church to "be transformed by the renewing of your minds" (Romans 12:2). He also offers a word of hope to some of us old enough to remember windup toys: "Even though our outer nature is wasting away, our inner nature is being renewed day by day" (2 Corinthians 4:16). Notice the enhanced sense of power these words have when they are hyphenated: re-member, re-turn, re-new. They re-mind us that God is able to do again whatever God has done before, if we will cooperate with heart, soul, mind, and strength.

In the early days of the eighteenth-century English revival the Reverend John Wesley observed that great movements of reform and revitalization seldom last long. He noted that the spiritual fires of the Protestant Reformation had grown cold even within the lifetime of Martin Luther. He feared the same for the new movement of the Spirit that he was leading. Near the end of his life, he wrote:

> I am not afraid that the people called Methodists should ever cease to exist either in Europe or America. But I am afraid, lest they should only exist as a dead sect, having the form of religion without the power. And this undoubtedly will be the case, unless they hold fast both the doctrine, Spirit, and discipline with which they first set out.[1]

The reality of decline and the necessity of re-turning to God are as old as the human story. And interest in producing turnaround is not limited to those who think in spiritual terms. We might say that the natural tendency of every activity and organization is to run down. Therefore, businesses, universities, community organizations, urban centers, and even individual persons need new beginnings or they expire. Thus, researchers in many fields such as economics, history, sociology, anthropology, and organizational development, as well as pastors, evangelists, bishops, and teachers have longed to know the secrets of turnaround. Although it would not be possible to explore all the models and theories of turnaround generated by researchers in these fields, one or two examples might reveal enough to show that similar dynamics are at work whenever new life grows in the face of death. Such a discovery should not surprise Christians who believe in "God the Father Almighty, Maker of heaven and earth."

From Research on Leadership

One of the best-selling nonfiction books of the 1980s was *In Search of Excellence: Lessons from America's Best-Run Companies* by T. J. Peters and R. H. Waterman. They observed the managing practices of forty-three organizations selected for their excellence. From several hundred interviews with employees they consolidated their findings into a list of eight critical factors or attributes that contribute to the success of organizations. Their list includes: (1) *having a bias for action*—encourage creativity and be willing to risk failure; (2) *being close to the customer*—have a genuine interest in meeting the needs of people; (3) *encouraging autonomy and entrepreneurship*—utilize the creativity of small work groups kept free from bureaucratic red tape; (4) *engaging productivity through people*—treat employees like adults with high expectations, direct communication, and plenty of affirmation for achievement; (5) *being hands-on and value driven*—formulate a belief system expressing clear, qualitative values; (6) *stick to the knitting*—focus on your best product, avoid getting spread too thin; (7) *using a simple form and lean staff*—keep the management structure simple, flexible, and stable; (8) *keeping simultaneous loose-tight properties*—maintain the tension between creative chaos and disciplined adherence to the values.[2]

In attribute 5 Peters and Waterman discovered seven consistent themes describing the underlying values of these organizations, including beliefs about being the best, valuing people as individuals, and the importance of using informality to enhance communication. To participate in one of these organizations is like being on a championship team, being part of a creative and caring family, or being involved in a pioneering adventure on a new frontier. These organizations are stimulating and contagious. They generate energy rather than deplete it.

From this research on excellence, Robert Waterman turned his energies to exploring how organizations successfully encounter change. Change is the one constant organizations face. It cannot be avoided. Only those organizations that are able to interpret what the changes will require of them and that actively manage the adjustments needed will survive with vigor. Without this ongoing renewal, there can be no ongoing excellence. The project looked initially at 500 companies in fifty-three industries. This field was narrowed to forty-five organizations, large and small, profit and nonprofit, that had faced the challenge of renewal successfully. The results were published in 1987 in Waterman's book, *The Renewal Factor*.[3]

Successful leaders of renewal he calls "builders" and describes them as persons who not only desire to make things better in the world but also believe they can. He contrasts these with "custodians" and "manipulators." Custodians are masters of inactivity. They dislike change. Under their leadership, organizations fail to recognize the changes taking place, fail to adapt, and eventually die. The manipulators, on the other hand, are extremely active, but they place their own ends above those of the organization. Under their leadership, organizations become mere gadgets in a game played by those who seek rewards only for themselves.

The behavior and personalities of the builders varied greatly, but Waterman identified eight consistent "dynamics of renewal" that they employed as leaders: (1) *informed opportunism*—quality information reduces the threat of surprise and enables flexible and intuitive planning; (2) *direction and empowerment*—management may establish the direction but everyone's input is valued; (3) *friendly facts, congenial controls*—contextual and factual information is welcomed because it allows decisions that anticipate change rather than just react to it; (4) *a different mirror*—habitual patterns isolate and entrench, but renewal leaders listen constantly to the best ideas available; (5) *teamwork and trust, not politics and power*—cooperation generates confidence and is more effective than competition and power politics; (6) *stability in motion*—renewal requires breaking old habits and empty patterns while maintaining stability through consistent beliefs, values, and vision; (7) *attitudes and attention*—renewal flows from attitudes and involvement that communicate attentive, confident optimism; and (8) *causes and commitment*—meaning in life emerges from a cause large enough to generate commitment by addressing human needs.[4]

These early studies in leadership addressing both the for-profit and nonprofit sectors have been enhanced through the years by multiple authors and variations on the theme. Writers like Stephen Covey, Peter Drucker, Warren Bennis, Robert Greenleaf, Peter Senge, Margaret Wheatley, and Jim Collins (to name just a few) have continued to expand our understanding of the nature and significance of good leadership. Hundreds of millions of dollars are made annually by those who become the best-known authors and publishers in this field, and surprisingly (or maybe not) almost of all of them recognize that things like humility, ethical lifestyles, character, and a servant's heart, along with vision and passion about life, are critical ingredients that make the difference when it comes to leadership.

Jim Collins, one of the best-selling authors and most sought-after speakers today on leadership, comments in his book *Good to Great:* "Greatness is not a function of circumstance. Greatness, it turns out, is largely a matter of conscious choice."[5] Collins goes on to describe the essence of the kind of leadership that makes the difference: "Good to great leaders seem to have come from Mars. Self-effacing, quiet, reserved, even shy—these leaders are a paradoxical blend of personal humility and professional will. They are more like Lincoln and Socrates than Patton or Caesar."[6]

Another leadership and management guru, Ken Blanchard, who coauthored the bestseller *The One Minute Manager* and over thirty-five other books on leadership, joined with a lifelong friend Phil Hodges in 2005 to package the greatest lessons they could find from "all time" and described them in their book *Lead Like Jesus.* The focus, like many other newer books on leadership, shifts toward being a "servant leader." The authors write: "To lead like Jesus, we must come to understand the spiritual dynamics of our relationships as both leaders and followers so that we may be agents of grace."[7]

Although some of these studies generally seem more couched in the language of business and management, the issues addressed are in many ways common to any human endeavor. Turning around a struggling congregation of Christ's church is certainly more than merely renewing or producing a good or great organization, but it is not less. Several of the themes described as renewal and revitalization strategies for businesses and corporations show up again in studies of revival and renewal movements in the history of the church, as well as in local congregations.

From Church History

One of the excellent studies of renewal movements throughout church history is *Signs of the Spirit: How God Reshapes the Church* by Howard Snyder.[8] In the introduction Snyder reminds his readers "that every renewal movement is, in some way, linked to others in history, and that somehow both sociocultural dynamics and the Holy Spirit are at work down through history."[9] His analysis begins with the late second-century First Charismatic Movement or New Prophecy Movement later called Montanism. The spiritual vitality and boldness of those involved challenged the authority and control of the established church. Conflict was inevitable. But conflict is almost always inevitable when the fresh wind of a turnaround movement is blowing.

Although Snyder takes a brief look at several other movements from the early centuries of the church, and offers an enlightening chapter on the theory of revitalization, the larger part of his work focuses on three later movements: Pietism, Moravianism, and Methodism. Aside from his own background, part of his interest in these particular movements is that they "were movements within large established church communions. These movements did not intend to start new sects, but to revitalize the established church."[10]

Gleaning the best lessons from these earlier movements, and hoping to offer a model of renewal for our day that "brings new life to the larger church without either compromising its own validity or causing a split,"[11] Snyder concludes his work with chapter 9: "Building a Renewal Strategy for the Local Church." He writes:

> The first and perhaps most critical beginning point for renewal is to understand that *the church has an inborn tendency to grow.* Growth is in its genes. Whatever its pathologies, every church has a vital urge toward its own health and renewal. The reason for this is simple, and simply profound: The church is the body of Christ. The very Spirit of Jesus is at work in his church,

always prodding and drawing it toward life and renewal. The key to renewal therefore is always a matter of identifying and removing the hindrances to vitality, never a matter of simply finding the right method, program, or success formula.[12]

While continuing to emphasize this inherent life force approach identified repeatedly in history, Snyder identifies ten strategies leaders need to practice when working for renewal in local churches:

1. *Begin with life.* Recognize and affirm the life and vitality already present in both individuals and structures.
2. *Don't attack entrenched institutional patterns.* If possible, bypass them and build new relationships and structures of renewal.
3. *Seek to pastor all the people.* Even those most opposed who resist persuasive argument can often be won over by demonstrated caring.
4. *Build a balance of worship, community, and witness.* Healthy churches reveal these qualities, and healthy churches grow.
5. *Provide small groups and home meetings.* The form may vary, but small groups meeting weekly are a critical ingredient for developing commitment to serious Christian discipleship.
6. *Affirm the ministry of all believers.* Teach the priesthood of all believers, offer training in discovering and using spiritual gifts, and free all persons to be in ministry for Jesus Christ.
7. *Move toward the biblical model of leadership.* Christian leadership only grows out of discipleship. Those gifted and called to leadership are called to equip others for ministry and to function as part of a larger leadership team for the congregation.
8. *Help the congregation discover its own identity.* Pastors are key to this "conceptual renewal" that allows each congregation to discover its own unique identity and mission within the framework of the gospel of the kingdom of God.
9. *Work to ensure that financial stewardship authentically reflects the church's mission and self-identity.* Finances are connected

to discipleship, not projects. God provides as we truly seek first the kingdom.

10. *Help the church catch a kingdom vision.* Although mentioned last, this is the most important. "Ongoing vitality is grounded in both the *vision* and the *practice* of consistent, continuous evangelism and compassionate, effective social transformation."[13]

As might be expected by those who have a strong creation theology, the principles discovered by Snyder and those discovered by Waterman, Collins, Blanchard, and others are very similar. Notice especially how similar is the emphasis on the importance of open and visionary leadership, the creative use of all persons' gifts, and the humble heart of a servant leader. Many of these principles or strategies will be seen again as we turn now to the reports of turnaround in small churches.

Turnaround Reports from Smaller Churches

What do the pastoral leaders in smaller churches we studied say are the key ingredients in bringing new life to their congregations? Their stories and descriptions of turnaround range from simple statements of faith in God to complex lists of plans and strategies; but all are marvelous reminders of God's amazing grace and available power.

Ray, a pastor in the Church of the Brethren, confessed: "We have done some things right and many wrong. We are a modern-day example of God's miraculous grace and restoration. Like Jericho, and like Gideon, we don't make sense; but when God's active, who cares!"

Bob C., a United Methodist pastor, reported: "I do not understand the changes we are experiencing. We evidently are doing all the right things without being aware. Our District Superintendent responded when I asked for some help in leadership training, 'You should be training others!'"

As I commented earlier, some aren't sure why things are turning around, they are just pleased and grateful that they are! Most often, however, the pastors of growing and lively smaller churches have a fairly clear idea of what they are doing to be co-laborers with God in bringing new energy and missional focus to their congregations.

J. R., pastor in an Assembly of God congregation, commented:

This is what God did in our depressed community. When I first came, God spoke to me, and I knew God was going to turn this community around. That first year we revitalized our facilities. The second year we visited. The third year we preached and prayed harder. God directed us to prepare for the recession, and we started a food bank. This year God is telling us to prepare for a window of opportunity for future evangelism. This is how we did it, by hearing what God was saying.

Bob E., wrote: "Foremost is a strong pulpit with meaningful messages. Next, I love my people and seek to meet their pastoral needs. Next, I enlist laypeople in doing ministry (first in Jerusalem . . . and then to the uttermost parts of the world)."

When describing the stages his congregation went through, he listed the following:

1. We made some definite physical improvements—cleaned, painted, rearranged, and so on.
2. We shared some "dreams" we had for the church in the next ten years.
3. We started a "Disciple" study group (and bragged about them and let them witness).
4. We "gathered" a choir (and bragged about them) and then started rehearsals (and bragged some more).
5. We invited music groups from neighboring communities to sing.
6. We built a plan for young adults—new class, nursery, and quarterly parties.
7. We established a "kids Club" for Sunday evenings.

Reverend Patty told the story of resurrection from a tiny church at death's door to a church full of hope:

Four years ago the conference and district were thinking of closing this church. It was a small church sharing a pastor with a large church. The pastor just didn't feel he had time to care for this church. It was run down and declining in attendance year after year and reached bottom at five [members in attendance]. Three years ago they decided (upon recommendation by another pastor and a friend of the little church) to separate this 152-year-old congregation from the larger church, make it a single-point charge, and have it served by a part-time local pastor. It would either survive or die—something like pulling the plug on a patient on life support systems. I was sent to pastor this "new" charge at that time. I have been blessed to be a part of it. Independence UMC is not only surviving, but thriving and growing. Thanks be to God!

In that first year we received ten new members, had a confirmation class for eight young people, and a new members celebration day, began our nursing home ministry, had potluck dinners, started special fund-raisers and an "outreach jar" to send money each month to a special need or cause. This church was "The Church" this past year. Their availability enabled the Holy Spirit of God to work in and through them. Thanks be to God!

Rose Sims, a great champion of reviving smaller churches, stuck with the simple but amazingly effective approach, used by her late husband, Oscar Grindheim, for turning around small, rural churches. Oscar was an immigrant from Norway who, after arriving in the United States, met and married Rose, and pursued his dream of bringing new life to dying churches all across the land—always as a bi-vocational pastor. Starting out in the American Baptist denomination, he was honored as their "Outstanding Rural Minister in America." When he and Rose moved to Missouri, they became Methodists and continued the work of "opening church doors shut as tightly as great coffin lids, after the mourners had gone."

> Time and again, three years after Oscar had stood at a tightly barred door, that church would lead the state in professions of faith and missions. Lives were miraculously changed by his undaunted faith in the Master Builder.
>
> Then, because churches of the quality he forged were always in demand, a full-time pastor would be appointed. Once again we would be standing at a lonely, nearly forgotten, nailed-shut church door. Time and time again, over twenty-seven years, Oscar proved that renewal could happen anywhere fishermen dared to battle the elements of neglect and discouragement and put out their nets for a catch.[14]

Inspiring imagery, but how did it happen? Rose Sims records Oscar's simple seven-step formula as "hard work, prayerful vigilance, evangelistic zeal for winning the lost, powerful preaching, willing counseling, adequate and attractive buildings and a pastor and people totally committed to Christ."[15] The "Grindheim formula" is simple and straightforward, but the strategies it represents have been highly effective in bringing struggling and dying churches to new life and vitality.

Thousands of similar stories are being told in multiple communities as smaller churches are experiencing turnaround. Our goal has been to learn from these stories and the people of these churches the lessons that might encourage and instruct others who are praying and working for a story of their own.

Twelve Emerging Turnaround Strategies

From the questions asked of the pastors[16] and the original interviews, it is possible to identify twelve critical tasks or strategies for turning around small churches. These are not listed in sequential order but in the order deemed most important by turnaround pastors.

Turnaround Strategies for
Small Churches

1. Enhance congregational confidence and hope for the future.
2. Stimulate concern for unreached persons in the community.
3. Engage in proactive and effective pastoral leadership.
4. Encourage an open, loving atmosphere in the congregation.
5. Clarify your own personal vision and be an example.
6. Help develop a clear, shared, congregational vision.
7. Work and pray for spiritual renewal among the members.
8. Provide high-quality preaching and inspirational worship.
9. Lead the effort to reach new people and grow.
10. Emphasize and practice prayer.
11. Develop new programs, especially for children and youth.
12. Plan to take risks and take them.

These twelve turnaround strategies emerged again and again in various combinations as both the pastors and the members of revitalized smaller churches told their stories. Pastors and other leaders of small congregations wishing to emerge from a season of decline and discouragement will do well to review this list carefully and invest wholeheartedly in those areas still needing particular attention.

What's to Come?

Like it or not, it is clear that pastoral leadership is critical to the turnaround process. Therefore, chapter 2 takes a look at the kind of pastors that make a difference. Chapter 3 explores the dynamics of bringing spiritual renewal to a congregation. Chapter 4 examines the major obstacles encountered and how they can be sidestepped or overcome. Chapter 5 looks intentionally at strategies for missional and evangelistic outreach and for church growth. Chapter 6 investigates how effective pastors lead their congregations to greater maturity in living together as Christian disciples. Chapter 7 takes a look at the challenge of pastoral transitions and offers several suggestions for the best ways to "keep the momentum going." Finally, chapter 8 offers a newly developed model to hold all of these ingredients together for the sake of *Turnaround and Beyond*.

When I was initially invited into these churches to listen to their pastors and lay members describe how God had brought them new life, the unavoidable conclusion that emerged was that congregational turnaround is ultimately a work of God's Holy Spirit. We are only privileged to play a part, but it is an important part. Yet, as co-laborers with God, "neither the one who plants nor the one who waters is anything, but only God who gives the growth. . . . For we are God's servants, working together" (1 Corinthians 3:7, 9).

Questions for Discussion

• What can we learn from the secular studies on renewal and leadership?

- Which of Howard Snyder's strategies for renewal are already most at work in your congregation? Which need to be given more attention?

- What recurring themes did you notice in the turnaround reports (pp. 9-12)?

- Which of the "twelve strategies" emerging from the one hundred turnaround churches are already most evident in your church? Which need more attention?

- What were the most helpful reminders or new ideas that emerged for you from this chapter?

CHAPTER 2

Pastors as Turnaround Leaders

Are we beginning to commend ourselves again?
Surely we do not need, as some do, letters of recom-
mendation to you or from you, do we? . . . Our
competence is from God, who has made us compe-
tent to be ministers of a new covenant, not of letter
but of spirit; for the letter kills, but the Spirit gives
life. . . . Since, then, we have such a hope, we act
with great boldness.   —2 *Corinthians 3:1, 5-6, 12*

C arl Dudley suggested years ago that pastoral leadership,
especially in smaller churches, is much more the work of
an artist than the work of a management technician. He
goes on to say, "The power of the pastor stems from the pastor's
willingness to walk with the congregation through the abyss,
through the mysteries of life. . . . Management skills can be
learned, but leadership is discovered in relationship to a group
who confirm the leader with particular authority."[1] Many
denominations and the pastors they ordain assume that authority is a kind of power granted by an institution, only to discover
that such authority is not necessarily recognized by the congregations supposedly benefiting from these "authorized pastors."
Contrary to Dudley's suggestion, however, pastoral authority
may not merely be something discovered or conferred by the
congregation either. Leadership authority, or power for effective

change, is a complex relationship between natural and spiritual gifts, personality, learned skills, and divine intervention.

The Apostle Paul had his own share of difficulties in being recognized as a fully qualified and authoritative apostle in the early church. In the passage from the Corinthian letter cited above, he reminds his hearers of the spiritual nature of his competence to be a minister of the new covenant. His authority is ultimately from God, who called him and equipped him by the Holy Spirit. Likewise, he writes to the church at Thessalonica, "So deeply do we care for you that we are determined to share with you not only the gospel of God but also our own selves, because you have become very dear to us" (1 Thessalonians 2:8).

How can skillful pastors who long for the resurrection power of God to be manifest in their churches learn to patiently guide a congregation through all the necessary stages of change involved in turnaround? The answer is love. Love is more an art than a science. It is a matter of Spirit and not merely a matter of letter or code. It is modeled after the Master Shepherd himself, who for three years patiently walked and worked with twelve disciples who frequently struggled to understand the new message and adjust to the messenger. When Paul was at his best, he learned how to be an imitator of Christ and bring the art of love's patience to the urgency of the gospel's task.

This is the same boldness and gentleness, urgency and grace that flavor the lives of pastors identified as "turnaround leaders." They have sometimes failed, and they have been misunderstood; but they have learned from their mistakes and have been encouraged by the Spirit of God. Through it all, they have grown to love their congregations and the communities in which they serve. Other things can be said about them, but nothing is more important.

Who Are the Pastors?

So, who are these pastors who make the right kind of difference in small churches and enable them to recover a sense of power and purpose? What are their gifts and training? How are they viewed by their congregations? What are their emphases in ministry? What have they learned the hard way—by making mistakes? What are their recommendations to other pastors serving in similar congregations?

Perhaps the natural place to begin is to look at their backgrounds and listen to their stories of being called and equipped to enter this ministry.

Personal Backgrounds

The turnaround pastors participating in this study came from ten denominations in twenty-seven states and Puerto Rico. They represented all regions of the United States, with the greatest representations from the Northeast (29%), the Southeast (27%), the South Central (12%), and the Midwest (11%). They ranged in age from twenty-six to seventy, with an average age of forty-seven. Eighty-seven were male, thirteen were female; a large majority were married (90%) and half (52%) had children living at home when serving in the churches we surveyed.

One interesting, although not necessarily surprising, fact was that only about 33 percent of these pastors had been involved in church since birth. Ten percent did not become members of a church until after they turned eighteen. Most (61%) were serving in the same denomination they entered as members and had been pastoring for an average of fourteen years, and the average tenure in their present church was five years.

Ministry Perspectives

When asked why they had entered the ministry, overwhelmingly they responded, "I was called by God" (70%). Other reasons for being in pastoral ministry included "personal fulfillment" (7%), "to preach the gospel" (5%), "to love God and do God's will" (4%), and "to help others know God" (4%). When asked to identify themselves with a theological label, they preferred terms like "evangelical," "moderate," "charismatic," or some combination of these terms rather than "fundamental," "conservative," or "liberal." They were also asked to locate themselves on a theological scale from liberal to conservative as compared to other pastors in their own denomination. Although most were not fond of such simplified theological categories, 15 percent saw themselves more liberal, 21 percent saw themselves in the middle of their denomination's spectrum, and 60 percent felt they were more conservative.

Almost 90 percent of these pastors reported a definite conversion experience. Most felt that this experience heightened their concern for others, or encouraged them to emphasize Christian witnessing and extend evangelistic invitations. When asked, "What is your motivation for being involved in evangelism?" three primary answers emerged. The first was described as an internal motivation based on the work of the Spirit and our new nature as God's children and Christ's disciples (21%). The second motivation identified was obedience to God's will (22%). The third and by far the most frequently mentioned motivation was the desire to bring to others the benefits of faith in Christ (57%).

Each of these motivations is clearly "Christian" and "biblical," and all three may only be facets of the same reality. Nevertheless, it is clear that most turnaround pastors preferred describing the motivation for their task in terms of the needs of others. People who describe their motivation for evangelism this way usually define successful ministry in terms of changed people. Persons preferring the "obedience" theme might be less concerned with "success" so long as they have been "faithful." Pastors describing their motivation as the natural outflow of God's love may resist evangelistic planning and prefer instead to leave everything to the leading of the Spirit. Perhaps additional research would show that we are looking as much at denominational doctrines as we are at individual preferences and personalities. In any case, the pastors in our sample desired changed lives and expected to see the transformation.

Preparation for Ministry

Earlier studies have indicated that full seminary education is not necessarily an indicator of effectiveness in serving smaller churches.[2] What kinds of preparation for ministry are most important when revitalized congregations are the objective?

Two-thirds of the participating pastors completed a master of divinity degree (MDiv) as part of their theological education. Forty-one seminaries were named, including institutions where denominational courses of study were pursued instead of academic degrees. Sixty-two percent of these pastors indicated that they had little or no training in evangelism prior to beginning their theological work. The 38 percent who did have such training reported it as being a combination of informal workshops, books, and hands-on experience. Fifty percent indicated they received no seminary course work in evangelism or church growth. Those who did have such courses ranked them as the most helpful for their pastoral ministry.

What Pastoral Gifts and Skills Are Needed?

Nearly every book written on ministry related to the small church emphasizes that relational skills are most important. The small church sometimes has been compared to a tribe[3] and at other times to a family.[4] In both cases the importance of the image employed is to remind pastors and other small-church leaders of the human dynamics and decision-making processes used by families and tribes. These smaller and intimate social institutions function quite differently from larger and more formal ones. Some "gifts and graces" for pastoral ministry are the same no matter where one serves. Others, however, seem to be uniquely important for effective ministry in smaller congregations.

When the participating pastors identified and ranked their own strongest qualities and skills for ministry, their top twelve answers were:

Gifts and Skills for Ministry

1. Preaching
2. Loving people
3. Working skillfully with people
4. Administrating and organizing
5. Teaching and training
6. Being a visionary and motivating people
7. Visiting one-on-one
8. Counseling
9. Leading by example
10. Living faithfully and loving God

11. Evangelizing
12. Being an energetic, hard worker

What kind of composite profile might emerge from this list? Pastors successfully leading small churches into new life and effective ministries of outreach and evangelism are excited about and feel competent in announcing good news from their pulpits. They love and understand people, and are comfortable with the patient task of building trusting relationships through affirmation, encouragement, challenge, confrontation, and good communication. They also like a sense of order and momentum. They see personal relationships as the foundation of the small church but not the only concern. They work hard and feel comfortable making decisions needed for the day-to-day and the long-range coordination of church programs and ministries. They especially like to sense that others are catching a new vision of the meaning of the gospel for their daily living, and they enjoy teaching biblical perspectives and training people in ways to invest this information.

Turnaround pastors know that people need a sense of how to see and shape their future. These good shepherds confidently lead the way to greener pastures. They do not, however, neglect to care for each member of their individual flocks. They visit them, offer counsel, and pray for them in times of trouble. They also intentionally reach out beyond the existing congregation to offer God's love and hope in Christ to others. They, in fact, are not going to ask others in the congregation to do things they are unwilling to do themselves. New life always means change, and change means taking risks. A deep sense of confident faith in the Lord, whose love and guiding presence is the same yesterday, today, and forever, is what inspires them to move ahead, no matter what obstacles may stand in the way. Because of their trust in the presence of the Holy Spirit, they have a contagious spirit of hope and endurance that does not falter even in times of disappointment.

Does this all sound a bit ideal? Perhaps it is, but the congregations served by these pastors are themselves living witnesses to this contagious life. Four of the churches visited as part of this study encouraged members to share their own observations of the changes in their church and the role their pastors played. Surveys were handed out to those willing to take a few minutes to share their ideas. One question asked was "What are your pastor's three greatest assets and strengths in ministry?" This is how the members evaluated the greatest "assets and strengths" of their pastors.

How Members Ranked Their Pastors' Gifts

1. Loving people
2. Displaying people skills
3. Preaching
4. Being a visionary and motivator
5. Having a personal faith and love of God

Also mentioned as important in approximately equal numbers, although less frequently than the above list, were the following:

Leading by example
Teaching and training
Evangelizing
Working hard, showing commitment and enthusiasm
Administrating and organizing

It is clear that the gifts and skills most noticed and valued by their members (with the exception of reversing "displaying people skills" and "preaching") are in line with the pastors' self-evaluations, namely: (1) loving and working skillfully with people, (2) preaching living and meaningful messages from the Bible, and (3) modeling a personal faith and offering a vision of hope. These are the contributions forming the core of pastoral leadership that enables endangered smaller churches to recover their sense of significance and effectively engage their communities with a living and powerful Christian witness.

How Do Turnaround Pastors Lead?

Although these pastors lead from love, they do lead. They are not just lovers. Or to say it another way, they do not value relationships and peaceful unity to the point that they will avoid conflict at all costs. They seem to be well aware that positive change demands the risk of initiative. These pastors list a congregational atmosphere of "love and acceptance" as the most important growth factor for their churches. But in second place they list "pastoral initiative." Or, to put it another way, they say that one of the most important factors impeding turnaround is, simply put, "pastors who don't lead." Pastors must lead if churches are to change.

There are today a multitude of models being offered as the true and most effective definitions and descriptions of leadership, both for the church and for secular institutions. The church has cycled through the nondirective "facilitator" and "counselor" models of the 1950s and 1960s, and the "coach" and "equipper" models of the 1970s and 1980s, to the "spiritual leader," "change agent," and "team builder" models of the 1990s, and now the "servant leader" models of the new century. And always in the background have been the models of "shepherd," "herald," "priest," "prophet," and even "king." How do the pastors in our study define their leadership?

When asked to portray the leadership role and approach they employed for revitalization and growth, most offered multiple descriptions of their efforts. For example, one pastor said, "visionary and catalyst as well as administrator." Another answered, "stabilizer, teacher, observer, exhorter." They seemed uncomfortable using any single term to define their pastoral leadership. Of the twenty-one categories identified, however, their top eleven answers were:

Leadership Role of the Pastor

1. Visionary
2. Enabler/Encourager
3. Partner/Friend
4. Facilitator
5. Cheerleader
6. Transformational leader/Change agent
7. Spiritual leader

8. Care giver
9. Manager/Director
10. Coach for success
11. Expert/Initiator

In reality, "visionary" stands significantly above the others, receiving a third again more votes than "Enabler/Encourager," and twice as many as "Partner/Friend." Whatever else these pastors do, they bring with them and plant in the hearts and minds of their congregations a vision of what can be.

Whether or not these pastors were familiar with the work of Warren Bennis and Burt Nanus, they manifested in their leadership much the same style these two researchers found after interviewing ninety outstanding CEOs and leaders in the public sector. Bennis and Nanus write:

> The study pursued leaders who have achieved fortunate mastery over present confusion—in contrast to those who simply react, throw up their hands, and live in a perpetual state of "present shock."
>
> The problem with many organizations, and especially the ones that are failing, is that they tend to be over managed and under led. They may excel in the ability to handle the daily routine, yet never question whether the routine should be done at all. There is a profound difference between management and leadership, and both are important. "To manage" means "to bring about, to accomplish, to have charge of or responsibility for, to conduct." "Leading" is "influencing, guiding in direction, course, action, opinion." The distinction is crucial. *Managers are people who do things right and leaders are people who do the right thing.* The difference may be summarized as activities of vision and judgment—*effectiveness*, versus activities of mastering routines—*efficiency*.[5]

Pastoral leadership, like any other kind of *effective* leadership, requires initiative that has a direction, a goal, a vision of what God wants to do and will do among us. For Jesus, the dominant motif was the establishment of the kingdom of God. What are the biblical images or themes most helpful to motivate and energize turnaround pastors? Each pastor was given the option of listing up to three such vision-inspiring resources. The result is 94 different favorites out of 230 votes cast. Those mentioned most frequently are listed below along with the number of votes they received.

Biblical Sources for Pastoral Vision

1. The Great Commission—Matthew 28:16-20 (27)
2. The body of Christ—Ephesians 4:7-16 (14)
3. Abundant life and the Good Shepherd—John 10:1-18 (11)
4. Pentecost—Acts 2:1-47 (10)
5. New birth and God's gift in Christ—John 3:1-17 (10)
6. God's activity in the early church—Acts (9)
7. Seeking and receiving the lost—Luke 15 (7)
8. Talents, and "to one of the least of these"—Matthew 25:14-46 (6)
9. Sermon on the Mount—Matthew 5–7 (5)
10. The work of the Spirit to make us witnesses—Acts 1:8 (5)

Some authors have observed that we have largely abandoned Jesus' own vision of the kingdom of God.[6] On the other hand, some would contend that facets of the kingdom of God are embodied, even if not mentioned, in each of these other images. Some believe both sides of this argument and are working to help churches cultivate once again the great richness and power found in the holistic vision of the kingdom of God.[7] In summary it might be said that the pastors surveyed have the following vision: the Holy Spirit is present in the church enabling all to sense they have a part in extending the abundant and new life brought by Jesus Christ to a world needing to be reached with a gospel that enables all persons to become fully committed Christian disciples.

What Were Their Pastor-to-Pastor Suggestions?

Our turnaround pastors were asked what suggestions they would offer to other pastors of smaller churches who were interested in evangelism and church growth. Their top twenty collegial recommendations were:

Their Recommendations to Other Pastors

1. Know and love your people.
2. Preach the wonderful gospel of Christ.
3. Pray and enable your people to pray.
4. Help your people reach out to others.
5. Help them dream of what they can be for God's glory.
6. Work hard; nothing comes easy.
7. Accept yourself and your people and "press on."
8. Be patient; new life grows slowly.
9. Hold on to and hold out your vision.
10. Celebrate the good that is happening.
11. Go ahead and risk new ideas and new programs.
12. Know and love God.
13. Teach God's purpose as found in the Bible.
14. Train people in evangelism and church growth.
15. Get yourself and others out visiting.
16. Take key people with you to training events.
17. Start with a committed core; don't wait for everyone.
18. Read about and study small churches that grow.
19. Set goals and move toward a strategic plan.
20. Delegate all you can and enlist new people.

These recommendations are not exactly steps, stages, or "the two-times-ten commandments" for congregational turnaround, but they do reveal once more how the twelve strategies mentioned in chapter 1 reappear in various forms as turnaround pastors share their hearts with colleagues committed to the same cause.

Learning from Mistakes

Meeting and talking with these pastors made it clear that they were not all cut from the same cloth, nor did they make everyone happy. Of course, neither did Jesus, Peter, Paul, Augustine, Aquinas, Francis, Luther, Susanna Wesley, or the most popular previous pastor. Making decisions and moving ahead is risky. Change means disagreements will emerge. Feelings will be hurt.

The definition and possession of power and influence will shift. Mistakes will be made by pastors as well as by parishioners.

When they were asked, "What mistakes have you made that have become 'lessons the hard way'?" their answers varied from "None that I can think of" to "So many I can hardly believe it." However, in God's grace these sisters and brothers indicated they were learning to accept their own human faults and frailties without being immobilized by them. Perhaps knowing ourselves in this way is the first step to being able to handle gracefully the problems that occur when others don't readily and wisely respond to our leadership. Another important "people skill" occasionally listed by the pastors as well as their members was a sense of humor. To be able to laugh at ourselves in those inevitable times of error or embarrassment is often the critical keystone needed to complete the doorway of trust and freedom that we must all walk through if we are to forge ahead into a new future instead of remaining behind in isolation and fear.

So, what lessons did these pastors learn the hard way? What does their confessional list of "mistakes" look like? Their top fifteen were:

Lessons Learned through Mistakes

1. I tried to do too much alone.
2. I was impatient.
3. I believed they would follow me before they claimed the vision.
4. I made decisions without waiting for the congregation.
5. I forced my vision rather than helping them discover their own.
6. I offered inadequate or no job training.
7. I overworked the dedicated few instead of reducing the pace or recruiting more widely.
8. I allowed myself to get negative and focus on the failures.
9. I misunderstood the meaning of members' actions and/or words.
10. I ignored the reality of original sin.
11. I didn't address problems or confront problem people early enough.

12. I ignored prayer and the comfort and guidance of the Holy Spirit.
13. I took other people's anger too personally.
14. I didn't pay enough attention to visitation and follow up.
15. I tried to please everybody.

Some of these "mistakes" are perhaps just inherent in being human—an interesting risk God took in the incarnation of Jesus. But notice that "timing" occurs as an issue in several of the items above. Generally, the pastors were of the opinion that they "rushed" things and moved ahead too soon without adequate preparation, training, or ownership by the congregation. However, they also realized they were caught in a predicament. There seemed to be no "perfect" time to move. Resistance never completely disappeared. One pastor acknowledged that just as soon as the congregation was over the last "fight" and were celebrating a victory, a new issue would arise and the tensions and questions would emerge again.

On the other hand, creative and energetic pastors are well counseled to be aware of their tendency to be impatient. Their own sense of satisfaction and success is usually tied to the changes they are working for in accord with the vision they have for the congregation's future. But timing and patience are much more important in small congregations than in large ones, and listening to the pulse of the congregation ought to be the job of the many and not just the one. It is a mistake to go it alone, trusting only one's own intuitions without checking with several honest friends in the church, including some who might disagree.

The goal is not to win battles or wars, but to enable a congregation to move as united as possible into its own new future. R. Robert Cueni, in his book *What Ministers Can't Learn in Seminary*, offers helpful wisdom on how to avoid a number of traps as ministers move away from their formal training into the world of the pastorate. Commenting on how to define "success," he writes:

> The church's primary concern remains the cure of souls, not management by objectives. When we are more concerned with meeting goals than caring for people, we have forgotten what it means to be the church.

It is, of course, important to keep measurable goals before the church. The church growth movement ably points to scriptural comments on the numbers of people joining the church. We deceive ourselves when we say we are concerned about people but fail to discuss numerical goals for the people we want to reach, the money we seek to raise, the programs we want to conduct, or the buildings we plan to build. . . . We must not, however, mistake the ends for the means. . . . The success of any congregation or pastor should be determined by what happens in the lives of those who are being touched by congregation and pastor.[8]

It took Jesus three years of ministry with a very small band of believers to know the right timing from his Father for his ultimate investment in the cure of souls. He often asked, "How much longer?" but until he had that answer, he demonstrated patient consistency. Pastors need to press on toward the mark of their high calling, but always with the cure of souls as their goal, and always with these words at work as a healing balm for their own souls.

Love is patient; love is kind; love is not envious or boastful or arrogant or rude. It does not insist on its own way; it is not irritable or resentful; it does not rejoice in wrongdoing, but rejoices in the truth. It bears all things, believes all things, hopes all things, endures all things. (1 Corinthians 13:4-7)

To the Turnaround

Pastoral leadership in smaller congregations is more an art than a science. We need to avoid the pitfalls and heed the time lines. But all these lessons are best learned by those who love what they are doing, love the One who called them into this crazy and challenging vocation, and love the very human brothers and sisters they work with for the glory of God's kingdom.

One of the important skills essential to effective turnaround leadership is knowing where the congregation is in relation to where it has been and where it is going. Several writers have addressed the stages or seasons of ministry in smaller churches. James Cushman, the Presbyterian small church and rural ministry expert, describes three stages of pastoral acceptance and leadership. The first stage focuses on establishing the primary relationship between the pastor and the people. He calls this the community acceptance stage. The second stage he describes as the season of fulfilling pastoral functions. Here the pastor is accepted by most of the people as their preacher, teacher, and counselor and is free to function well in these areas. This is the time to begin working creatively for program planning and development. The third stage begins when the pastor is accepted as a full community participant, as much a part of the larger community as anyone else. This normally comes as the congregation is extending its mission intentionally into the community. This progression of pastoral acceptance and leadership authority often takes five to seven years in Cushman's experience.[9] Others who may be more optimistic have described this process as taking three or four years. Whatever the actual time frame, the reality is that fully functional and productive relationships take time to develop.

We will examine more closely the idea of stages of change in the next chapter as we explore the processes involved in leading a congregation to "turn toward the spirit," a turning that is critical if a church is to find a new sense of faith, power, and confidence.

Questions for Discussion

• What characteristic of the pastors in the *Turnaround Study* most surprised you? Why? Which ones seemed most expected?

• When you think of biblical images or passages that are most important to your congregation, which ones come to mind? How do these inform the way your church bears witness in your community?

- In the list of recommendations given on p. 25, which ones are already most at work in your congregation? Where do you think more attention should be given? Why?

- Trying new things almost always means making some mistakes. Which of the mistakes listed on pp. 26-27 are most like your own tendencies? How does your congregation deal with those who make "mistakes" like these?

- Several studies indicate that both loving patience and focused vision are important in leading smaller-membership churches to renewal. Which would you say is most important in your congregation right now? Why?

CHAPTER 3

Turning toward the Spirit

*Take care, or you will be seduced into turning away,
serving other gods and worshiping them, for then the
anger of the Lord will be kindled against you and he
will shut up the heavens, . . . and the land will yield
no fruit; then you will perish quickly.*
                                       —Deuteronomy 11:16-17

*You foolish Galatians! Who has bewitched you? . . .
Having started with the Spirit, are you now ending
with the flesh? Did you experience so much for
nothing?*   *—Galatians 3:1, 3-4*

A Look at the Problem

It is not a new problem for the people of God to turn away
from the Spirit and ignore the counsel of God. Probably each
of us knows the problem personally, as well as having noted
its presence in local churches and whole denominations. Through
the centuries God has sent prophets, apostles, reformers, and
even come himself in Jesus to call us back to our "first love," and
rekindle the flame of the Holy Spirit in our midst. It is clear, however, that the established religious people, who thought of themselves as on God's side, frequently did not respond well to the
voices of these messengers. Thus, leaders today with similar

goals in mind ought not to be surprised if their voices are not immediately welcomed by all who hear.

The early church, even in the days of wonderful, pentecostal freshness, had to face the problem again and again. As early as the fifth chapter of Acts, Ananias and Sapphira demonstrate how easy it is to "play along" without truly being committed to the vision or sensitive to the presence of the Spirit. Peter had to confront them and remind the whole church of the dangers of lying to God and living a double-minded life, as James later called it. In fact, both New and Old Testaments are filled with very similar counsel and correction.

Were it not for trouble in the churches Peter and Paul founded, we would have a very small New Testament, if we had any at all. So, it could be said that churches struggling with strife, party-spirit, spiritual coldness, loss of love for widows and orphans, lack of courage, no desire to risk the dangers of bearing witness, and immorality in all its forms are in good company and just part of that great line of splendor. Church work, and the work of the church, both demand that we face squarely the reality that although sin and death have been defeated through Christ's death and resurrection, they both still have a lot of wiggle in them.

All the problems faced by churches, especially today's smaller congregations, however, cannot be easily traced to such traditional understandings of sin. Many kinds of changes have taken their toll through the years. Most smaller congregations in the United States are located in rural areas and small towns. Economic and social shifts during the last several decades have not been particularly kind to these communities. Many have experienced significant population loss or radical shifts in ethnic and cultural makeup. Most often, the old mainline denominations have declined in both members and number of congregations in these settings, but frequently, independent churches starting new works in these contexts have actually realized significant growth. One of the main problems for the established congregations is the cost of supporting a full-time pastor and his or her family. These costs have risen dramatically in the last few years, especially related to costs for health care, and many smaller churches are spending more than 50 percent of their budget simply to support a pastor.[1] In addition, the problem of frequent pastoral changes has denied smaller churches the continuity of leadership so important to long-term church growth.

Smaller, rural institutions of all types suffered losses through most of the last century. Schools, banks, businesses, and family farms were forced into consolidation. Historic smaller towns all over the country have boarded up most of what is left of their "downtowns." It is quite an accomplishment that most of the churches in these communities have survived at all when so many institutions around them have collapsed, closed down, or consolidated. No wonder the number one ailment of smaller congregations today, according to many studies, is the problem of "low self-esteem." In fact, by an almost two-to-one margin, pastors confirm that negative self-image is the number one problem facing smaller churches.

A survey of laypersons in The United Methodist Church highlighted another side of this social and spiritual malaise. Clark Morphew, an ordained clergyman and columnist for the *St. Paul (Minnesota) Pioneer Press*, wrote:

> Only 3 percent of respondents said they want their pastor to have the following positive characteristics; competence, independence, determination, courageousness, maturity, fair-mindedness, dependability, forward-looking attitude, imagination and ambition.
>
> More than 40 percent of those taking the survey said they want their pastor to be cooperative, caring and honest. Those are all good characteristics to have if clergy are simply expected to maintain the status quo.
>
> But if clergy also are expected to drive the congregation's mission forward or shape public opinion or make the church grow, there had better be some courage in the preacher's soul. [2]

On the very day that I write this, I have had a telephone conversation with a pastor of thirty years' experience who was "fired" by the elders of his church while he and his wife were on vacation and informed he would not be allowed to return to the congregation for either worship or discussion. The elders were frightened that he wanted to make changes beyond their comfort zone and force them into what he called "renewal" and "turnaround."

The problem of conflict will be examined along with other obstacles on the turnaround path in chapter 4. But for now, the issue is the larger challenge of what a pastor can do to help shift the tide from helplessness and hopelessness to courage, empowerment, imagination, and confidence—no small task. In fact, the change must be supernatural. Turnaround pastors are quick to affirm they do not produce this change; rather, they lead their congregations into the presence of the risen Christ and pray and wait for the Holy Spirit once more to transform struggling and defeated disciples into men and women of radiant hope.

Turning to the Spirit

In his book *Signs of the Spirit,* Howard Snyder gleans the ages of history for principles of church renewal and revitalization. He suggests five different, but interrelated, dimensions of renewal that are important if new life is to come to a church.

1. *Personal Renewal*—a dramatic, decisive experience or simply a deepening that gives greater peace and joy. . . . Nothing can substitute for this. First through the new birth, then through the deepening work of the Holy Spirit, God wants every son and daughter to know the joy of deep, fulfilling communion with himself.
2. *Corporate Renewal*—a dramatic spirit of revival sweeping the church, or simply by a gentle quickening of the church's life. . . . A renewed congregation is more powerful in God's hands than a collection of isolated Christians.
3. *Conceptual Renewal*—God gives a new vision of what the church can and should be. . . . Conceptual renewal comes when our models are challenged, and we are forced to rethink what the church is really all about.
4. *Structural Renewal*—simply finding the best forms, in our day and age, for living out the new life in Christ. . . . *Any* traditional form, structure, or practice that helps us be alive and faithful should be kept and improved. Any that insulate us from the fresh fire of the Spirit should be modified or retired.
5. *Missiological Renewal*—A church needing renewal is focused inward. A renewed church focuses outward to mission and service in the world. . . . Sometimes renewal actually begins here.[3]

Snyder acknowledges that new life may begin in any of these five areas, but for it to be long lasting, faithful to God's purpose for the church, and dynamic, it must integrate all five dimensions.

Turnaround pastors engage in a vast array of personal and programmatic efforts to assist their congregations in the process of drawing near to God and letting God draw near to them. But six important ministry arenas can be identified, which contribute significantly to Snyder's five dimensions of congregational renewal. The six renewal arenas are: (1) personal pastoral effort, (2) prayer, (3) special events and spiritual retreats, (4) Sunday worship and preaching, (5) small groups, and (6) community involvement.

1. Personal Pastoral Effort

In the last chapter we learned of the special love reported by these pastors for their people. Love does not work well from long distance or in the safety of isolation. The very heart of the good news of Jesus Christ in the doctrine of the Incarnation is that "God so loved the world that he gave his only Son" (John 3:16); and this Son so loved that he gave "his life a ransom for many" (Mark 10:45). Jesus repeatedly sought to prepare his followers for ministry in his name by reminding them what good shepherds do (Luke 15:1-7; John 10:1-18) and how to function as loving servants (John 13). Any pastor unwilling to be such a shepherd-servant is in danger not only of vocational failure but also of God's judgment.

> Therefore, you shepherds, hear the word of the LORD: As I live, says the Lord GOD, because my sheep have become a prey, and my sheep have become food for all the wild animals, since there was no shepherd; and because my shepherds have not searched for my sheep, but the shepherds have fed themselves, and have not fed my sheep; . . . hear the word of the LORD: Thus says the Lord GOD, I am against the shepherds. (Ezekiel 34:7-10)

Pastors who lead their flocks like good shepherds do not see their work as a way to make a living, but rather a way to joyfully offer up their lives in service to God and God's sheep—both the ones already gathered and those in need of being sought out and brought home. It is appropriate, then, that pastors who lead their

congregations to turnaround offer as their number one suggestion to other shepherds of smaller flocks: "Know and love your
people."

In practical terms, what does this look like, and how does it
contribute to congregational renewal? For one thing, it means
these pastors stay. When one member of a revitalized congregation in Pennsylvania was asked what his pastor did to help it happen, he simply answered, "He stayed! He stuck it out. The last
two or three just couldn't take it and they left." I asked, "What is
the 'it' they couldn't take?" He replied, "You know, the pressure:
not having everything the way they wanted, people not agreeing
with them, just the stuff you'd have at any church." Good shepherds have thick skin but tender hearts and gentle hands. They
aren't easily discouraged; they sense God's call to the particular
parish they are serving, and they plan to stay for as long as it
takes. For many of them this has meant sacrifice, and there is
always the danger of self-pity. But for those who stick it out with
joyful hearts and confidence in God's guidance, there is the wonderful reward of seeing miracles of *personal renewal* in the lives of
others and *corporate renewal* for an entire congregation.

A second aspect of their pastoral care is they pay attention to
people and help them believe they are valued and important.
They "visit, visit, visit" as one pastor said when asked for suggestions he would offer to other pastors. They encourage persons
during times of stress and pain but also as a way to invite them
to risk trying things they haven't done before. They know how to
say "Thank you!" and "Great job!" and "Sure you can!" They stop
by, make phone calls, and send notes. Jim Sparks, who pastors a
Church of God Congregation in Battle Creek, Michigan, reports
never experiencing a problem with divisive conflict in his
churches. Years ago, he began the practice of writing notes of
"remembering you in prayer" as well as appreciation and affirmation to his members—five notes a day, each week. In eleven
years his congregation has grown from eighty in attendance to
nearly 450, and all of his current staff (including a secretary and
maintenance manager) practice the same discipline of personal
hospitality, prayer support, and gratitude expressed through
notes sent in the mail.

Members of the churches studied say things about their pastors like "She's warm, welcoming, knows you are there, and is fun to be with" and "You always feel like you are important to him, but then so is everyone else too." And these pastors seem to know how to find new and important things for people to do. One fairly shy young woman was discovered to have artistic skills and a great love for children. The pastor encouraged and worked with her until she was willing to try presenting the Sunday morning children's sermon. Eventually she created an entire illustrated book of messages for children and submitted it for publication. Recognizing, affirming, and employing for God's glory the gifts and graces of others is a critical first-level ingredient in establishing a sense of hope and potential for a congregation's future. Discovering and employing people's gifts in ministry not only changes their personal lives but also frequently contributes to *conceptual, structural,* and even *missiological renewal* for the entire congregation.

A third important ingredient for renewal through personal pastoral effort is a life that reveals both spiritual spontaneity and discipline. These pastors read, study, pray, and work hard; yet they know how to prioritize their families and take time off. Although they are patient about the timing of renewal, they are constantly exuding confidence that God is already at work bringing it to pass. They seem to have a twinkle in their eyes as though they know that a secret surprise party is just about to break on the scene. However, their reservoir of personal spiritual vitality is not a secret, and they let people know that they are dependent on the living water drawn from the well that never runs dry. They make time for soaking in the pages of the Bible, and they take days away on personal spiritual retreat just to walk, pray, ponder, and listen. Many of them take time every week to announce they will be in the sanctuary praying for the needs of the congregation and the community. Some invite others to join them for these times but only if they come to pray. Although they have plenty of new ideas because of their reading and research, they don't simply try to reproduce someone else's program. Doing so can be, and frequently is, disastrous. They instead seem to talk about, pray about, and preach about the unique "new thing God wants to do right here with us." *Conceptual* renewal catches fire in turnaround churches because the wind of the Spirit fans the sparks of expectation struck by their pastors.

There is no way around it. Pastors are on a stage being watched as a kind of preview to the main event. As time goes by, other kindred souls will emerge with the same twinkle in their eyes, or will at least be hungry for the change to come. These persons often form the initial informal network of support for the pastor and, like the first fruits of springtime, reveal a foretaste of the harvest to come. One pastor revealed just such confidence when he said, "Most small churches have much more to offer the world than they think they do; and if I can awaken the spirit of even a few in a small church, it makes a big difference."

Personal pastoral effort establishes the spiritual climate and culture in which renewal can grow. The busy activities of *personal, corporate, conceptual, structural,* and *missional* renewal all need a kind of peaceful center. The shepherd is not that peaceful center, but he or she must point to it and live in it or renewal has little chance of becoming a reality. Like it or not, pastors are important; and their personal effort as caring, loving, freeing, exploring, praying, praising people sounds the trumpet that God has come to meet us.

2. Prayer

Prayer is usually the starting point for *personal renewal* for members of the congregation, just as it is for the pastor. Jesus carefully reminded his disciples of this in the image of the vine and the branches: "Just as the branch cannot bear fruit by itself unless it abides in the vine, neither can you unless you abide in me" (John 15:4). Most of us have a tendency to think this means something like "keep believing and keep working." But it really is much more like "stay connected to me as I have stayed connected to my Father." The vine and branch image reminds us that "fruit" is what God produces, for we only bear it on God's behalf. Living the Christian life and being productive for God are not things we do. It is what the Spirit does in us as we first and foremost keep our lives connected. How? One way is through faithful attentiveness in prayer.

Prayer opens the windows of the soul. Prayer acknowledges that God alone is able. Prayer is not what we do when we've already done all that we could. Prayer is living constantly in the awareness that it is "not by might, nor by power, but by my spirit, says the LORD of hosts" (Zechariah 4:6). Prayer is what links us to God's active presence. How can there be any personal or corporate spiritual renewal without prayer? According to most of the pastors surveyed, there can't be.

One of the most amazing stories of *corporate* spiritual renewal and growth is the story of Union Chapel United Methodist Church in Muncie, Indiana. This 130-year-old congregation moved twice in ten years in order to find enough space for the multitudes who had come to participate in its ministries. In 1983, worship attendance averaged seventy-eight. Today, almost 2,000 people are worshiping regularly in a renovated automobile showroom. Gregg Parris, the pastor, has many gifts for ministry. The members of the congregation affirm his personal integrity, his preaching, and his teaching. But most evident in their descriptions of what led to the turnaround and their amazing growth is that Gregg called them to prayer. One member, remembering the major transitions from being a small, plateaued, traditional congregation to a megachurch said, "Gregg began spending a minimum of one hour daily in prayer himself, then encouraged the rest of us to join in that commitment. It has changed lives, and our church will never be the same."

Prayer is not only a channel for personal and corporate renewal, it also contributes significantly to conceptual and missiological *renewal*. Bandana is a small farming community tucked away in the fertile bottomlands of the Ohio River in western Kentucky. A church there lamented its declining attendance and decided to send representatives to a countywide training event on evangelism and church growth. Their pastor wrote:

> The next week we held our own church growth meeting. We discussed each of the recommendations of the earlier meeting. One by one we ruled them out because we felt they didn't fit our situation. Since we didn't know what to do to bring about spiritual renewal, we decided to pray for guidance. The seven people at that meeting decided to challenge the congregation. To our surprise, eighteen people committed to come to the church and pray. So we prayed for a month, coming to the church at all hours.

> The first result of the prayers was this: People noticed a change in themselves. One member got up in our Sunday school assembly and said, "I've never prayed for thirty minutes at one time. And I want to tell you, it's changed my life." The second result was a change in the direction of our program planning. It seemed that several ideas became right for us. At some point, it began to dawn on us that the Holy Spirit was helping us. Ideas began to come and we didn't begrudge the extra time spent at another meeting at church. And when we started to implement these early ideas, we found continual help. People appeared out of the woodwork. We are convinced that the foundation of revival lies in seeking the guidance of the Holy Spirit through prayer.

Perhaps prayer relates to structural renewal only in the sense that "form" is supposed to follow "function." Once a congregation discovers a new purpose or "function," it needs new ways to organize in order to accomplish the required ministry. Small groups demand small-group leaders. Mission teams require coordinators. A new choir, a second worship service, or a community-wide ecumenical food pantry often requires structural renewal if the vision is to become reality. The early church discovered this in Acts 6:1-7 when seven new "deacons" were added to the apostolic leadership in order to care for a whole group of neglected believers.

Few in our churches today realize the missiological dimension of prayer. Prayer is a ministry of its own. One of the most unusual and effective models of missiological renewal through prayer came from the Linda Vista Presbyterian Church in San Diego, California. After a merger effort with another congregation failed, this small church led by a retired Air Force chaplain invested what they had been learning about prayer into a community outreach program called DIAL HOPE. Twenty-four hours a day, upwards of 5,000 calls a year came in to the DIAL HOPE telephone answering machines at the church. Those who called during the week received a prerecorded daily devotional, and on Sundays, a recorded sermon was also featured. The callers were invited to request prayers for particular needs. A Discovery Prayer Group, as well as the entire congregation, prayed for the requests, which were printed every Sunday in the bulletin. Their pastor reported:

The main thing is, the program works. *It reaches people who need our Lord.* . . . You reach handicapped people, troubled people, people living far from your church, working people and retired people, elderly people and others who are confined and need the Word of God to uplift them. . . . And although the DIAL HOPE program is an outreach program, we have found it helps not only those in need but church members as well. It has stimulated Linda Vista members to witness for their Lord.[4]

This was not the only outreach program of the Linda Vista church, but it became the one that best identified them as a congregation that trusts in God and cares about the needs of all people. Surely such an identity is close to the heart of being "turned around."

A good friend who took the step in midlife to become an ordained pastor in the Presbyterian Church USA began her first session meeting with her elders suggesting that they take a few minutes to pair off and share with each other in prayer. Nothing happened. She clarified her instructions, but no one moved. Then one of the elders said to their new pastor, "We don't have time for this kind of thing. We've got lots of business to take care of, so you just pray and let's get started." It wasn't easy to change the culture of that congregation to one that valued prayer. But when she left after seven years of serving that little church, prayer was taking place everywhere and in all kinds of groupings. Life in that congregation had changed, and their outreach ministries to many persons had produced growth in membership, programs, and spiritual life. It was no longer a "small church."

In her book *Unbinding the Gospel,* Martha Grace Reese summarizes the national four-year "Mainline Evangelism Study" funded by the Religion Division of the Lilly Endowment. She reports this kind of resistance to serious investment in prayer is encountered again and again. But it also became clear in this study that the few congregations that had exciting success in reaching new adults with the gospel had rediscovered prayer. Reese writes:

After years of talking with pastors and laypeople in churches that are thriving, and in churches that are failing, I am clear that the only way to do ministry successfully, to lead a church or to live a life in today's United States, is to pray deeply. We must hand ourselves over to God in clear-headed, accountable, no-naïve prayer. We need to rely as much on God for pragmatic guidance as we can stand! Without God vividly in the mix, we drift, life declines.[5]

What if there are indeed things that God withholds from us unless and until we follow Jesus' counsel to "ask" and even engage in "much prayer"?

3. Special Events and Spiritual Retreats

The importance of special evangelistic events and programs does not rate as high among turnaround pastors as some might expect or may have been the case in previous generations. What is interesting, however, is how often both the members and the pastors affirmed a special event as important to their own renewal.

Some pastors did arrange for a gifted colleague or evangelist to come lead a revival or special weekend. Others preached their own. But what these special occasions were designed to accomplish from the outset was primarily a "turnaround" for the members of the congregation, not strictly an evangelistic event for the unchurched. The importance of prayer in the story of Union Chapel in Muncie, Indiana, was mentioned earlier, but the start of their revival is recorded in an article written to help newcomers identify the turnaround point of God's activity in their midst.

> A few prayer warriors began to pray for a Spirit-filled pastor to be appointed to what was at that time the two-point charge of Union Chapel–Millgrove. Gregg and Beth Parris accepted the appointment.
> In October, revival services were planned. A fellow United Methodist pastor was scheduled to preach four nights but had another commitment on the final evening, so Parris preached the revival service that night. At the end of the service, revival broke out . . . and the Holy Spirit began to move in a mighty way.

One of the "prayer warriors" was discouraged that nothing much had been happening. At the end of the service she stepped forward and shared her heart wondering if there was something more she should have been doing to allow the Spirit of God to come. She knelt at the altar to pray. After a moment of quietness, from the back of the church her husband stood and announced that he thought it was about time he became a Christian. Parris, aware that this man and his wife had been long-term members of the church, was confused. He asked for clarification and the man replied, "I thought I was pretty clear about what I said." His pastor asked him if he had ever truly repented of his sins and asked Jesus to be his personal Lord and Savior; and he confessed, "Not really, but I want to tonight." What a reminder of the difference between being active in church and surrendering one's life to God through Christ! The Spirit of the Lord had arrived, and not only was the congregation set on a new future, community members heard the word of the new life going on at Union Chapel and began to take notice. It was a new chapter of Acts being written.

There seems to be an understanding among these pastors that God often uses special events and special witnessing and preaching to stir the coals of a congregation into a rekindled fire. In addition to such stories about revivals and preaching missions, it was interesting to note the continuing influence of the Lay Witness Mission movement, and the program variously known as Cursillo, Tres Dias, De Colores, and the Walk to Emmaus. Several pastors wrote about this special retreat program in their reports, and others mentioned it in conversation over the phone or in person. One pastor had more than half of his congregation involved in the Emmaus renewal movement sponsored by The Upper Room in Nashville, Tennessee.[6]

Although this is no place to offer a long and detailed description or evaluation of this program, perhaps a brief introduction is in order. The model originated in Catholic parishes in Spain in the late 1940s. It began to make its way into Protestant circles in the United States in the 1960s and 1970s. By the early 1980s, The Upper Room in Nashville had developed its own ecumenical version and named it The Walk to Emmaus after the image of downcast disciples walking blindly with the risen Lord to Emmaus until their hearts were strangely warmed and their eyes were opened as he broke the bread (Luke 24). Men and women attend separate weekends (Thursday night to Sunday night) where they are led by a team of about twenty-five laypersons and clergy, usually representing several churches and denominations, through an intensive seventy-two-hour reminder of the basic ingredients of living in Christ. Outstanding music, excellent food, inspiring talks on grace and Christian living, engaging small-group discussion, times of prayer, Communion, and other acts of worship and reflection round out the weekend. A great variety of renewal experiences is reported by those who have attended. The stated purpose is to be an instrument of the larger church to assist local congregations in the development of Christian leaders. The primary approach, however, is not what would normally be called "leadership training." Rather, it is an experience of immersion into a community of grace where Christian essentials are rehearsed and new visions of the kingdom of God and the renewing love of the Holy Spirit are offered.

Pastors who are willing to open themselves to such special events and encourage their members to become involved find that people revitalized in the loving grace of God want to do something about it. They want others to experience what they have discovered. They want to offer themselves in sacrificial service to others. Larry, a United Methodist pastor in Pennsylvania, tells of a man in his congregation who returned from an Emmaus weekend and said, "What job do you need done that nobody else wants to do?" Larry answered, "Mow the lawn in the cemetery." He added, "It's looked like a green patch of heaven ever since!"

Special events and programs of spiritual challenge and refreshment can play a significant role in the process of renewing a congregation. Wise pastors and lay leaders who serve in smaller churches recognize they do not have to be isolated from the larger body of gifts and graces that Christ provides for all of his church. We are not sent to build our own little kingdoms but to joyfully celebrate and utilize all the gifts the Lord has given us through others, and "grow up in every way into him who is the head, into Christ, from whom the whole body, joined and knit together by every ligament with which it is equipped, as each part is working properly, promotes the body's growth in building itself up in love" (Ephesians 4:15-16).

4. Sunday Worship and Preaching

Leander Keck writes:

> Renewing any institution requires revitalizing its core, its reason for being. Unless this core is refocused and funded afresh, renewal becomes a matter of strategy for survival. Accordingly, the churches' renewal becomes possible only when their religious vitality is energized again by a basic reform of their worship of God.[7]

The renewal of churches is not the same as secular endeavors when hunting about for a strategy. Rather, it is what happens when the people of God "repent," when they "turn away" from all their other forms and fashions, and stand before Almighty God with mouths and souls full of praise to the One who is worthy. Worship is not a strategic means to some other end; it is the end itself, the goal of our living and dying. And, Keck adds, "In the praiseful worship of God, the role of preaching is vital. In fact, renewal, preaching, and praise belong together."[8]

Almost every book published on ministry in the smaller church has at least one chapter on worship or preaching. Several years ago Will Willimon and Bob Wilson worked together to produce *Preaching and Worship in the Small Church*.[9] More recently, Laurence Wagley,[10] David Ray, and Robin Wallace and Terry Heck[11] have contributed to this special arena of spiritual life for smaller congregations. Whether or not the preacher or the worshipers in revitalized churches ever read any of these authors, they definitely know worship is central, and they pray it will be significant.

The pastors in our study confirmed this. When asked what their congregations did best, they responded in ranked order: (1) love and accept others, (2) prepare wonderful meals, and (3) worship the Lord. When asked what factors contributed most to the growth they experienced, they mentioned: (1) love and acceptance, (2) pastoral initiative, (3) new programs and ministries, and (4) alive, open worship. When asked, however, what they did best, they ranked their roles as preachers (1) and teachers (5) much higher than their work as worship leaders (16). Yet they perceived that the various elements of worship such as prayer, music, celebration, openness to God, love for one another, and preaching God's Word all work together to make the Sunday morning service the most important single cause of renewal and turnaround in their churches. More than in any other way, it is in worship that smaller congregations turn to the Spirit and find new life.

David Lattimer, a scholar-leader in a small denomination in the Midwest, undertook extensive research to determine which churches in his tradition were most effective in reaching new persons for Christ. As part of his research, he visited churches as a participant observer. Five of the churches (group A) had had the highest number of professions of faith the previous year. Another five (group B) had none. Reporting on preaching in these churches, he writes:

> I experienced the preaching as excellent in two of the group A churches and good in the other three. Two of the sermons were 15 minutes or less in length, while the other three averaged about 30 minutes. In group B one sermon was good, while three others were weak. Of the three weak sermons, one was very negative, in another the pastor read a sermon from a periodical, and in the third the pastor apologized for his sermon. In the fifth church of group B the pastor refused to preach and insisted that I do it.[12]

Commitment to good preaching makes a critical difference. And more and more turnaround preachers are leaving their notes and manuscripts behind, moving away from their pulpits, and learning to communicate biblical truths through the medium of stories and modern parables.

One young pastor and preacher credited this frightening and yet empowering new style of preaching with much of the sense of renewal both he and the congregation experienced. When he was first contacted by a denominational leader and asked to consider moving from the staff of a larger church in Ohio to pastor a struggling Church of God congregation in a tiny crossroads community in Pennsylvania, he responded, "I'm not much of a preacher." But he learned. He reported, "In seminary I was taught to preach from a manuscript. That's all I knew. I tried it for eight years. But four years ago I shifted to using only notes, and then to stories and no notes. It has radically changed my experience and effectiveness as a preacher."

Many prepare for preaching by reading both the lectionary and works of contemporary Christian poets and storytellers. The goal is to create totally thematic worship and preach the biblical message focusing on one point, leaving the people with the sense that they have had their minds and eyes opened to God. Worship teams of four to six persons meet together weekly to plan and pray. Music becomes more and more focused on helping the congregation join together in praising God. Drama or children's puppet presentations may be used from time to time, and a sense of joyful delight in being the body of Christ in the presence of God permeates the sanctuary.

In worship, personal and corporate renewal happens. Here, under the inspired and anointed preaching of biblical yet contemporary messages, conceptual and missiological renewal is set in motion as a new vision of being God's people and doing God's work is taught and caught. It is from this kind of worship—alive, open, prayerful, Bible-centered, expectant, participatory, joyful, God-focused—that the flame is rekindled.

5. Small Groups

It has been argued by some that the small church *is* a small group; it doesn't *have* small groups. In reality, however, any time a small church has a group that gathers other than for worship, it is supporting some form of small-group emphasis. Something happens when three, six, or ten people gather to talk and pray and read from the Bible.

Although there are many reasons people join together in small groups (12-step programs, age-level fellowships, sharing and prayer groups, ministry teams, recreational teams, committee meetings, choir practice, and so on), the most common is Bible study.[13] For some it is the standard "Wednesday Night Bible Study." Others spoke of special short-term opportunities or longer-commitment resources like *Encountering God, Witness,* or the DISCIPLE Bible studies. In the course of several months together, those who engage in this type of focused fellowship find themselves deeply renewed in their love for one another and for the divine vision given through the pages of Scripture.

James Cushman created a model to bring conceptual and missiological renewal to the Presbyterian church he pastored in West Virginia. He wrote: "The pastor is a teacher, . . . but a pastor cannot force and direct this process of growth in people. This must be a natural process that occurs as people in a congregation learn how to study the Bible and theology together and reflect upon their own life situation."[14] After serving as their pastor for four years, he began a year-long program aimed at congregational recommitment. In the spring he selected a task force of four persons to work with him over the next nine months on the design and a trial run of the proposed six-week small-group study process.

In January of the following year, members of the task force became leaders of four small groups. The congregation and inactive members were all invited to participate in six weeks of exploring the Bible, reviewing the meaning of church membership from The Book of Church Order, evaluating the meaning of having a personal belief system, and considering the practical implications of such a faith. Following the meetings, each group outlined its own composite statement of what it meant to be a church member. After a church-wide dinner in March where each of the groups reported, a writing team was selected to compose the new statement of membership commitment to be used on Easter Sunday.

Cushman reported:

> One result of the study program was an immediate increase in the level of commitment, interest, and participation on the part of a number of persons in the church. . . .
> Any small church that is involved in a process of revitalization needs to be engaged in study in order to discover new directions and new identity. As that new direction and identity emerges, the congregation is then ready to begin planning how it can achieve its mission.[15]

Recognizing that smaller-membership churches face a different kind of challenge in forming small groups than do larger congregations, a research team at Church Innovations spent three years (after an original, more generic study of seven years) to create a special resource for churches averaging forty to sixty in worship. *The Small Church Small Group Guide* is not so much a small-group program or a lesson series as it is a carefully crafted set of principles emerging from the research. It recognizes the special relational dynamics of smaller congregations and the biblical and historical values for spiritual development emerging best in small groups. In summary, the seven principles presented are:

1. *The Principle of Synergism:* When individuals work together, they can accomplish much more than they could separately.
2. *The Principle of Learning Retention:* Group discussion allows people to ask questions, share doubts, explore applications, and hear additional insight.
3. *The Principle of Transformation:* Deep, lasting change is not a quick or easy thing, yet the call of our faith is to be transformed by God. Many people experience this in a small group.
4. *The Principle of Risk-Taking and Experimentation:* Most congregations are not in the practice of taking risks and are afraid to try. This is where small groups can help. . . allowing people to explore and experiment with new and possibly risky ideas and interactions.
5. *The Principle of Problem-Solving and Decision-Making:* A well-run small group can make better choices than individuals can by themselves.
6. *The Principle of Support and Belonging:* One of the best ways to meet persons' need to belong or be included within a community of faith is to have some type of small group for them.
7. *The Principle of Accountability:* Many people credit true friends, ones that held them accountable through a long process of struggle, for their ability to persevere and reach their goals.[16]

The form of small groups in turnaround churches may vary, but their impact for both personal and corporate transformation is beyond debate. Like the early church, whose members gave themselves to "the apostles' teaching and fellowship" (Acts 2:42), congregations are being turned around today because disciples are committing themselves to these same disciplines as they meet together in our modern-day versions of both "the temple" and "from house to house."

6. *Community Involvement*

Normally, the progression of new life in turnaround churches is from some combination of personal and corporate renewal to conceptual and structural renewal and finally to missiological renewal. But a growing number of both individuals and congregations are finding the key to turnaround begins with mission to others.

In a society increasingly composed of aging baby boomers and their offspring, discovering a meaningful mission to invest one's life in is often a truly life-changing experience. More and more older, second-career persons are entering seminary in preparation for some form of full-time Christian ministry. Why? For some it is because of a wonderful new personal and corporate experience of spiritual renewal through their local church or a program like the Walk to Emmaus. Others find their renewal begins through a short-term experience with Volunteers in Mission, or Habitat for Humanity, or helping with a local effort to address the needs of the homeless, or traveling across the country to assist in hurricane or flood relief. They are tired of "playing church." They want to feel they have given something of themselves to others in need. They seek, in Erik Erikson's terminology, the experiences of generativity and life integrity. It is more blessed to give than to receive. Many baby boomers and a growing number of younger generations are at a point in life where they *need* to give, not to get.

Typical of this pattern is this comment from a pastor in Texas.

> *Working with people in the poverty of villages in Mexico taught us dramatically the meaning of loving our brothers. . . . It was almost with a feeling of reluctance that the team picked up and left on Saturday morning. We had become very close to one another, and we had functioned well and accomplished much as a team. We had spent a week together doing hot, dirty, and hard work. Most of us had only one shower all week long. We ate very simple food. But yet, we enjoyed one another's company.*
>
> *We had a feeling of accomplishment and satisfaction of a job well done. We knew that there was no way that we could*

satisfy all of the needs; however, we at least had done something. We had done more than just write a check. We had put the rubber to the road in the name of Jesus Christ.

In this experience we learned that what is most important in life is not what we want to do. The most important thing in life is what God wants us to do, and that is to serve other people in the name of Jesus Christ.

This type of missional renewal helps many congregations develop an innovative and cooperative network of support for persons seeking assistance with all kinds of life challenges. It leads some churches to begin ministries to help people recover from drug and alcohol addictions. Others provide food, counsel, and support groups for people who are in financial and housing transitions. These pastors and the members are experiencing the Holy Spirit's power in many areas, but they are learning above all that turning to the Spirit means doing what the Spirit says. Missiological renewal causes many to raise questions about the meaning of their faith and the power of the gospel. Personal and corporate renewal can follow; and frequently, conceptual and structural renewal are very close behind. The order is not what is most important. The fact that all areas or dimensions of renewal are in place is what makes the lasting difference.

Turning Points and Curves

Some smaller churches involved in turnaround can remember absolute turning points when spiritual life rushed in to change almost everything from that day on. These are largely the exceptions, not the rule. Most churches experience spiritual renewal as a mostly unperceived unfolding of grace at work through many channels. It is only later in looking back that they realize all that was happening.

Howard Snyder's five-dimensional model of congregational renewal is a helpful framework to keep in mind as new life in the Spirit is sought and found. Renewal is a total fabric and not merely working hard to design a mission statement, or change the organizational structure, or have individuals experience a wonderful weekend. But nothing is more at the heart of ongoing spiritual refreshment than what happens Sunday after Sunday during worship. Other ingredients may contribute to rekindling the flame in a small church, and several have been mentioned. But a pastor who loves to praise God and joyfully preach the good news, who expectantly prays for the Spirit to come and heal the broken and reclaim the lost, and who unashamedly loves God and the sheep of God's pasture will be an instrument the Lord will use to restore a vital hope and a bright future to almost any local church.

It is a great calling. It is a great gospel. It is a great hope. And so with our brother Paul, let us pray for ourselves and all the churches of God:

> For this reason I bow my knees before the Father, from whom every family in heaven and on earth takes its name. I pray that, according to the riches of his glory, he may grant that you may be strengthened in your inner being with power through his Spirit, and that Christ may dwell in your hearts through faith, as you are being rooted and grounded in love. I pray that you may have the power to comprehend, with all the saints, what is the breadth and length and height and depth, and to know the love of Christ that surpasses knowledge, so that you may be filled with all the fullness of God. (Ephesians 3:14-19)

Questions for Discussion

- God's people have often faced both internal and external challenges. What are the greatest challenges faced today by your congregation? What solutions do you think are needed?

- Howard Snyder identifies five dimensions of congregational renewal. Which one of these is already most at work in your church? Which one is most in need of improvement?

- Very few smaller congregations will experience new life without strong pastoral leadership. If you are a pastor, what are the most important contributions you bring to turnaround? (If you are not the pastor, offer your perspective as a member.)

- Emphasizing congregational prayer, vibrant worship, and small groups seems closely associated with turnaround. How would you explain this?

- How does your congregation best reveal to your community a love for God and a love for neighbor?

CHAPTER 4

Overcoming the Obstacles

*Rev. Moore persisted; nearly the entire choir and its
director quit. . . . A number of families left the
church.*[1]

*At the end of forty days they returned from spying
out the land. And they came to Moses and Aaron and
to all the congregation . . . and showed them the fruit
of the land. And they told him, "We came to the land
to which you sent us; it flows with milk and honey,
and this is its fruit. Yet the people who live in the land
are strong, . . . and to ourselves we seemed like
grasshoppers."*

—Numbers 13:25, 27, 28, 33

The people of God through every age have been confronted
by "giants" of various names that drive many into fearful
retreat, divide God's people against themselves, and create
the feeling for most everyone that they are little more than
grasshoppers. When the armies of King Saul were immobilized in
battle because they feared the Philistines and their giant warrior,
Goliath, it took the unconventional approach and the courageous
faith of a lad named David to free the Israelites from their
bondage. David was absolutely confident of one thing: "the battle is the LORD's and he will give you into our hand" (1 Samuel
17:47). When the spies sent out by Moses returned from the land

of Canaan, there was a majority report and a minority report. Those frightened that they could not succeed in crossing into the promised land cried out against their leaders, and "said to one another, 'Let us choose a captain, and go back to Egypt'" (Numbers 14:4).

John Bunyan's classic tale, *The Pilgrim's Progress*, reminds us that following the guidance of "Evangelist" to "yonder shining light" and the narrow gate of salvation is dangerous and costly. "Christian" discovers that staying on the rough and narrow way is difficult—at times, almost impossible. But Christian Pilgrim knows this is what he must do to obtain his salvation. And although he encounters many distractions, false friends, and deadly beasts, he also is led each step of the way by true friends sent from God who know how to sidestep the obstacles and lead him to the Celestial City. This is the kind of friendship, guidance, and encouragement needed today in multitudes of smaller churches all around the world. This chapter listens as "true friends" guide us around, over, and through some dangerous obstacles and on to the prize of our upward call.

Identifying the Obstacles

Although all the obstacles faced by smaller churches are too many to mention, some problems seem to show up repeatedly. Turnaround pastors in our study who had successfully overcome many such snares along the path listed their top ten.

Obstacles Facing Turnaround Leaders

1. A lack of vision for doing God's will
2. A defeatist attitude draining energy from people
3. Members attached to old ways and ideas
4. Inadequate finances
5. Inflexible older members
6. Inadequate or rundown facilities
7. Low levels of faith and commitment
8. A cold shoulder toward outsiders
9. Power cliques that create conflict
10. A survival mentality

When they are listed separately, it is clear that some of these threatening "giants" are related. For example, at least three items are related to the attitude and self-image of the congregation (2, 7, 10). Two items focus on the need for a vision of the future rather than dwelling in the past (1 and 3). Two items deal with conflict between members or the pastor and some members (5 and 9). Two items are related to financial issues (4 and 6). And, although all of this could readily present barriers to "outsiders," there is the specific problem of being "cold" and "closed" to them (8).

As a way to double-check the problems faced by small churches, the pastors were also asked, "What three primary factors do you think most impede smaller churches from becoming revitalized and engaged in effective ministry and evangelism?" The ten most frequently mentioned are listed below.

Factors Impeding Revitalization

1. Low congregational self-esteem
2. Fear of change and taking risks
3. No vision for the future
4. An "us versus them" attitude
5. Power cliques in the church
6. Lack of finances and/or stewardship
7. Apathy and burnout
8. Pastors who don't lead
9. Closed to "outsiders"
10. Unwilling to work hard

With the exception of the order they are listed in, and item 8, the two lists look almost identical. Notice that although there are plenty of giants "out there" such as major societal/cultural/spiritual shifts, economic challenges, high mobility of populations, and newer megachurches down the road—just to name a few— isn't it interesting that all of these are "internal" giants or obstacles, not external ones? Maybe, after all, they are the ones we can best address.

Thus, we can identify five major problems faced by churches and their pastors as they seek to move from a survival mentality to renewed investment in ministry and mission. The problems are: (1) low self-esteem and apathy, (2) a lack of vision for the future, (3) a lack of concern and love for "outsiders," (4) finances and stewardship of resources, and (5) issues of power and interpersonal conflict. Various forms of these five "dragons of defeat" may raise their ugly heads along the pilgrim path to congregational renewal, and the sequence of their appearance may vary. But let there be no mistake, these are the real giants in our day that need to be confronted by any pastor seeking "to proclaim release to the captives and recovery of sight to the blind, to let the oppressed go free, to proclaim the year of the Lord's favor" (Luke 4:18-19).

Staying on the Path

Mercifully, pastors do not always need to fight all of these dragons at once, and they do not have to fight them by themselves. In fact, on occasion, the pastors report they are the beneficiaries of the work of others who went before them. Eugene in South Carolina described how each of four pastors contributed to the congregational momentum that led to their turnaround. Ten years before he arrived, a colleague had "pushed" the congregation toward change. His lack of patience, however, created more tension than could be tolerated and he was asked to leave. A second pastor came to "heal the wounds." Eugene states:

> He worked diligently to draw the people together. He helped them celebrate the ministries they had and led them to see how they might expand their ministries into other areas. He also helped them feel connected to the rest of the denomination in a way they had not before. During this time they were able to sell the old, inadequate "Mill House," which had served as the parsonage for many years, and purchase a new parsonage close to the homes of many of the members. The youth program became seen as a way to reach out to the community, and a new van was purchased to be used both for the youth and the senior adult group.

An emergency situation elsewhere led to a new appointment for this pastor and a retired interim pastor came for ten months. Eugene continues:

He agreed to visit the sick and shut-ins, and the congregation agreed to divide up responsibilities for worship leadership. Each group took turns—the youth, the women, the men, and the seniors. All that this meant to the congregation is yet to be explored, but I am sure this was when a new sense of accomplishment, unity, and confidence developed.

It was after this interim pastor's ministry that Eugene arrived.

In the fifteen months since my family has arrived we have begun building on the work of the former pastors. I have a strong sense that we need to develop a vision statement as a congregation. We have spent a great deal of time in meetings discussing who we are and where we need to go. A special new planning committee has been appointed and is working hard to study our building use and building needs. At present we are planning to build a larger fellowship building where the church and the community can gather and share in shaping our future. I believe my job is to help our congregation discover their own hidden dreams and find the means to fulfill them as the people of God.

Few pastors work in isolation from the whole history of a congregation. There are those who have gone before and there will be others who follow. Although it can be painful and discouraging to watch progress made during one tenure of leadership experience a setback following a pastoral change (a problem to be addressed in chapters 7 and 8), the words of Paul are as critically important for us today as when they were written to the Corinthians in the first century.

What then is Apollos? What is Paul? Servants through whom you came to believe, as the Lord assigned to each. I planted, Apollos watered, but God gave the growth. So neither the one who plants nor the one who waters is anything, but only God who gives the growth. The one who plants and the one who waters have a common purpose, and each will receive wages according to the labor of each. For we are God's servants, working together; you are God's field, God's building. (1 Corinthians 3:5-9)

In other words, we may not always play exactly the same role for every congregation we serve. What worked last time may only frustrate things this time. If the planting has already taken place, only watering and weeding are needed. To blindly start at the same place in each new pastorate is the height of arrogance and insensitivity to the Spirit of God.

But when the church has had a major disruption, it is well to note how the "together" language and actions described by Duane can show the way to lead a church to health and wholeness.

> The church had a major split a year before I arrived. Together we decided that this congregation needed to work at unity, forgiveness, and change. We decided each step together and openly. A newspaper was started so that every member would be aware of all that was happening and of future plans. I have had no major problems in six years.

What would it look like to start from scratch following the list of major obstacles and impediments to renewal listed by the pastors in our study? It would require first of all that there be a healing of the past and a movement toward healthy congregational unity otherwise known as "faith, hope, and love."

1. Recovering a Sense of Grace

In much of the literature, "self-esteem" is listed at the most critical problem faced by smaller churches. Lyle Schaller identified this "grasshopper mind-set" years ago.

> While it is seldom mentioned, a very significant factor behind the lack of numerical growth in many small congregations (especially among those urban churches that today are only a fraction of the size they were back in the 1950s or 1960s) is the low level of corporate self-esteem among the members. Frequently the members of these congregations see themselves as small, weak, unattractive, powerless, and frustrated with a limited future. That self-image often creates a self-perpetuating cycle that produces policies and decisions that inhibit the potential outreach. Their priorities are survival and institutional maintenance, not evangelism.[2]

Many things contribute to this problem: insensitive and untrained leaders, community and demographic changes, conflict between members or families in the congregation, inadequate income, aging buildings, loss of members, and rapid turnover of pastors, to name just a few. Smaller churches, where relationships are most important, quite naturally experience insecurity, doubt, and even anger because of this turnover. One pastor writes, "I was the fifth pastor in five years. I had to persuade and show them my willingness to stay and to love and to serve the church."

What is needed to enable a congregation to escape this pit of self-pity? The answer is a renewed sense of the grace of God. But a word of caution: no one ought to try to pull another out of quicksand while standing in it. Pastors anxious to throw a rope of rescue need to make very sure they are secure themselves. Whether young or old, whether experienced in pastoral ministry or not, the most important quality is one's own inner sense of faith, confidence, and self-worth. It is easy to get dragged in and dragged under. Some become frightened when they are not immediately successful, and they flee—perhaps wisely so. There is no need for any more casualties than absolutely necessary. Success cannot be defined by any one effort. Sometimes we "fail" if our goal is to always be just the right person for the job, or if we look through short-term spectacles. Paul and Silas were not a big hit in Philippi when they first sought to bring the gospel there (Acts 16), but eventually the church at Philippi blossomed so that Paul could say, "I thank my God every time I remember you, . . . confident of this, that the one who began a good work among you will bring it to completion" (Philippians 1:3, 6).

One second-career pastor, looking back on successfully helping a church regain its vision and grow during his first seven years of ministry, wrote:

> *Ministers going through this must expect some hurt and pain. This kind of growth can be scary and threatening. The minister can become the whipping post. It is not personal, but it hurts just the same. Often I thought of moving; however, I needed to stay, become part of their hurt, and facilitate the growth. In two or three years this church will be over the hump; and I would be remiss not to add, the praise and glory for all this belongs to God.*

Another pastor from Louisiana counseled:

Expect little or no real support from the church at first, rather expect skepticism, cynicism, and no desire for growth. Therefore, expect to do a lot of early work on your own. Be prepared for the unexpected, perhaps a volunteer will show up to help visit. Each church will be different as to the type of evangelism that will work; a revival at one, knocking on doors at another. Be prepared to be innovative, as in making room for more Sunday school classes when there is no room. Don't be disappointed if there are no results right away; and don't compare your "accomplishments" with other pastors.

Once the "reality check" on a pastor's ego and expectations has been run, what practical steps can be taken to help a negatively charged or passively resigned congregation regain a solid footing in God's grace and be energized for their future?

First, turnaround pastors counsel others to "control what you can, not what you can't." Learn to lead from personal strengths with a positive approach. Don't attack the resistance, but announce and demonstrate a grace-filled gospel. Be convinced of God's call to your particular congregation, and share their sense of "honor" in being placed there by God for the wonderful things that are to happen.

Second, to help create a sense of openness, they suggest that one should "be open." From Ohio, Dennis wisely advises: "Set the pace by being open yourself, and open your parsonage to your people. Have them share how they came to faith and/or to this church, what they like, and what they would like to change. Begin where your people are."

Third, visit everyone, listen, and, when appropriate, share your own faith story and dreams for the church. Meet with any group that will have you. Look for opportunities to meet with a men's breakfast group (formal or informal), a women's circle, the youth—even if there isn't an official youth fellowship. Take them for an outing.

Fourth, make sure you serve as a pastor working from a theological and faith base, not merely as the manager of an institution. One pastor commented: "Without the grace of God, humankind is on a course of self-destruction at all levels. God has called me to help people discover their sacred self-worth in him that they will never see apart from Christ. I believe that God wants people to be whole again, healed from the brokenness of sin." See the people as Jesus did and have compassion on them as Christ's shepherd (Matthew 9:35-38).

Fifth, learn to respect, affirm, encourage, and compliment everyone you can for anything you can. Bob, a pastor in Florida, counseled:

> *The respect of a congregation is the first step in restoration. Our idea of who they are becomes to them the hope and pattern of what they may become. Congregational elevation to self-respect requires a great deal of work on the individuals within the congregation. Respect the refuse collector as much as the banker and vice versa. Jesus did this, and he taught it to Peter and the other disciples. To restore a church from lostness to effectiveness, we must work on the individual's and the congregation's self-respect at the same time. We must learn the art of giving sincere, honest praise. Do not condemn, criticize, or complain. Show them a better way.*

This is not just an approach to interpersonal relationships. Share with others in the congregation the good things that are going on. Post achievements, birthdays, anniversaries, news items, and thank-you notes on the bulletin board. Tell the old-timers who have given their best to the church for decades that you know how much they have done.

Sixth, whenever appropriate and possible, attract recognition from outside. Get a newspaper writer to cover some special event, or write the article yourself and submit it. Include a photograph whenever possible. A picture is still worth a thousand words, or more. Invite denominational officials to come visit without an agenda except to enjoy worship and thank God for this congregation.

Seventh, involve the congregation in worship and preach messages designed to reveal the grace of God at work today. Earlier we noted that worship is the centerpiece of spiritual renewal. But worship truly needs to be the work and joy of all God's people. Invite members of all ages to participate. Make it the whole family sharing together in the presence of God. Ask one to share a testimony, another to sing a song, or lead the prayer, or read the Scripture, or bake the bread and help serve Communion. And when it's time for the message, Willis from Arkansas caught the spirit of grace-full narrative preaching when he proposed:

I used stories from the Bible about people being used of God even when they were small and powerless in the face of difficulty. I emphasized the truth of being new persons in Christ. We are important. I had them try one thing at a time. Their confidence grew as they experienced success.

Eighth, help them experience success and celebrate a victory. Richard suggested: "Love them and lead them. Give them what they need—change—not what they want. How? Don't give up. Start and complete small programs to emphasize progressiveness. Applaud areas of change and growth and then challenge the next step in the process." Patty was appointed as a part-time local pastor to a dying church with an average attendance of five. She described some of the steps forward:

We had a workday at the church and twenty-five people came. We got a lot done and surprised ourselves. Then we finished a project that had been hanging in the balance for five years (a new outhouse and a parking lot). I rang the church bells for the first time in ten years.

This was a church learning to celebrate the grace of God and to catch a vision for new life.

2. Imparting a New Vision

When the turnaround pastors were asked how they overcame the obstacles, by far their number one answer was to teach and preach a new vision for serving God. The goal of becoming a turnaround church is not merely more money, more activity, more members, and more goodwill. These might all be signs that something good is happening, but there is a need for every congregation to clearly recognize its identity as the church of Jesus Christ planted by God for the benefit of all who can be reached by its ministry and message of salvation.

According to the J. B. Phillips translation of the New Testament, the first letter of Paul to the Thessalonians begins:

To the church of the Thessalonians, founded on God the Father and the Lord Jesus Christ, grace and peace from Paul, Silvanus and Timothy.

We are always thankful to God as we pray for you all, for we never forget that your faith has meant solid achievement, your love has meant hard work, and the hope that you have in our Lord Jesus Christ means sheer dogged endurance in the life that you live before God, the Father of us all.

We know, brothers, that God not only loves you but has selected you for a special purpose. For we remember how our gospel came to you not as mere words, but as a message with power behind it—the convincing power of the Holy Spirit. You know what sort of men we were when we lived among you. . . .

You have become a sort of sounding-board from which the Word of the Lord has rung out.

(1 Thessalonians 1:1-5, 8 JBP)

What difference might it make for members of a congregation to spend time reading these verses and then ask themselves: "What is our church founded on?" "What does that mean?" "How much prayer is being invested for our church?" "What has our faith, hope, and love meant?" "Do we know God loves us?" "What is our special purpose?" "Can we remember how the gospel first came to us?" "How do others see the effectual power of the Holy Spirit in us?" "How does the Word of the Lord ring out from us?"

Helping impart a congregational vision is not the same as working out a strategic plan or writing a mission statement. It is more a matter of "seeing" things the way they are intended to be, and can be, and will be, by God's grace. What can a pastor do to help clarify and empower this vision?

First, pastors who lead congregations to find a corporate vision have a personal vision already at work in their own lives. They believe in a personal God who intervenes in history and changes people. Their own experiences of conversion or their call to ministry are vivid and they are thus convinced that God is ready and able to touch the lives of others. Greg wrote from New York: "The Holy Spirit is God's gift for the church. Jesus and the healing touch of Jesus in my life brings a constant confirmation of the power of this reality in the face of every challenge." Hal from Alabama told his story this way:

I was truly lost in the world of living for money and material things when I realized I was sad and lonely within myself. I had tried everything else to discover satisfaction, but only when I said yes to God did I begin to experience the real substance of life. It has given me a sense of joy knowing that there is real hope for all persons in finding Christ as Lord of all.

Second, preach and teach the redemptive and loving activity of God and the purpose of God for the church. Avoid moralisms and lessons on the oughts. Focus first on what God does before emphasizing our response. David, who pastors in Alabama, put it this way: "Develop a vision based on God's ability, not human ability. The best days of the church you serve are always ahead, not behind. Immerse yourself in God's word and pray seeking him. Wait on his response, then go with it. The results are his concern." Along the same lines, Kirk from Wisconsin commented:

One important emphasis is that we try to help people see themselves and their church's mission in the pages of the Scriptures. For example, the day we bought our new site, we erected "12 stones" in the worship service (Joshua 4). The day we dedicated the new site with a worship service outside on the site, we celebrated the completion of our journey to "The Promised Land," and allowed everyone there to sign a "Pilgrim Roll." Help your people find themselves and their church in the Bible. They are there.

Third, "re-member" and celebrate the heritage of the church. Every church has a story and a history. The Holy Spirit has been active in the lives and events of the past. Carl Dudley dedicates a whole chapter to the power of this kind of remembering in his book *Effective Small Churches in the Twenty-First Century.*[3] Many churches recover a sense of their heritage and identity by telling the old stories in new ways (a drama, a written history, a heritage quilt, stories about the memorial gifts, a special series of "Heritage Days," old fashioned testimonies of "I remember when God . . ."). Joseph DiPaola, for his D.Min. project, used testimony, letters, narrative, and photographs to compose the story of faith of the church he was then serving. Then he published it. In the preface he writes:

> I hope you will both enjoy and be encouraged by what follows, and be able to discern within its pages the gracious leading of God, who has been calling, testing, refining, and transforming lives after the image of Christ in and through a particular community of people now known as Wissinoming United Methodist Church.[4]

To remember what God has done among us in the past, even though we were not perfect, can encourage people to dream dreams and see visions for the future.

Fourth, provide intentional and structured opportunities for members to voice their dreams and visions, perhaps a day apart with leaders or during a series of Sunday evenings. One pastor shared: "We have a day apart for planning and fellowship. It helps them see the whole picture. Two members asked me, 'What do you mean the best days are in front of us?' We shared with them our vision. They picked up the vision and began to get excited about their potential."

Fifth, ask good questions. Ed from Arkansas reported, "I surveyed the congregation with questions that would cause them to think." An example of such questions and a way to ask them is modeled above with the J. B. Phillips translation of 1 Thessalonians 1. Other questions recommended included: "Whose church is this?" "Why are you here?" "What business are we in?" "How's business?"

Harold Percy, rector of Trinity Anglican Church in Streetsville, Ontario, and founding director of Wycliffe College's Institute of Evangelism, made it a practice for years of asking pastors two questions: "What's your job?" and "How do you do it?" He has broadened the questions for congregations: (1) "Why are we doing what we are doing?" and (2) "Why are we doing it the way we are doing it?" He calls these the foundational questions for the "essence and mission of the church." He then adds three focusing questions:

> The first is, In the lives of those we're seeking to reach, what do we want to see happen as a result of their coming within the

sphere of influence of our ministry? . . . The second question is, What are we offering that from their point of view would make it worth their while to get involved with us? . . . The third question is, What price are we willing to pay in order to be able to reach them?[5]

Sixth, work together to arrive at a common vision of what God is calling the congregation to be and to do. The answer might come out as simple as one sentence, or a phrase such as "Making room for our neighbors in the fellowship of faith" or "A warm church that shows the love of God and ministers to all people in a fresh New Testament atmosphere." Or, it may be more like what Russell Springs United Methodist Church in Kentucky worked on for a year: "Our purpose is to develop faithful followers of Jesus Christ by bringing people to Jesus and membership in His family, building them up to Christlike maturity, training them for ministry and sending them out in mission in order to magnify God's name."

Seventh, as the congregational vision becomes clearer, begin to establish priorities for investing your own gifts and energy in light of congregational expectations and the vision. A judicatory leader and pastor in New Hampshire wrote:

> The "Setting of Priorities for Pastoral Ministry" exercise made me aware of how I as a pastor have assumed people in my parish know my concepts of ministry and are aware of my efforts to carry these out in day to day activities. It seems there is inadequate communication between pastor and people relating to what we do on the "other six days of the week." This is not to say we need to punch a time clock or fill out "monthly reports" including each day's activities, but we do need to share what we do with our people and let them know how we vision our ministry.

His own list goes something like this: (1) people, (2) preaching, (3) worship services, (4) visitation, (5) unchurched families, (6) small groups, (7) pastoral counseling, (8) new leaders, (9) saying no, (10) "In times of change, rearrange!" As a pastor more clearly establishes his or her priorities in line with personal giftedness, God's call, and the congregational vision, others will recognize that "adjusting" is what all of us do as we follow the leading of the Holy Spirit into a new and brighter future and reach out to others, offering Christ.

3. Extending Concern to Outsiders

Any time a family is facing its own internal struggles with damaged relationships, guilt, feelings of betrayal, loss of income, death of a family member, or stress from any number of causes, the tendency is to pull in on itself. Fewer friends are invited over. Every new challenge, even the small ones, feels like a burden too heavy to carry. Depression can set in. Conflict is always just below the surface, or exploding out into the open. As time passes, some healing may take place. But unless real forgiveness and redemption are experienced, it is not likely that this is going to be an ideal home for foster children, or the best place for a son or daughter to live after a divorce, or a haven for a widowed mother-in-law to find love and comfort.

Healthy families are wonderful gifts of God because they offer the energy of faith, hope, and love to one another and to many outsiders who just "happen by." The love and respect spill over into the world around and invite response like the wagging tail of a small puppy. Families in the midst of blaming one another or under enormous stress do not seem to offer the same welcome. They are like wounded insects curling inward on themselves. People may notice, but most won't want to stay and watch. A small church is like family. When it is emotionally and spiritually healthy, it is very attractive. When it is turned inward in anger and pain, or self-preoccupation, it is not.

How can pastors and church leaders help small churches turn their survival-focused fears into excitement about reaching out to others?

In the first place, turning toward the Spirit, recovering grace, and imparting a new vision need to be under way. It could be said that once love and the power of the Spirit are moving again to heal those who have waited a long time for hope, the natural direction for the flow of energy and love is outward toward friends and family. This is not a simple "one, two, three" approach, since even though new people are seen as desirable to help carry the load, there is also the fear that they will take control and change things. Based on his pastoral work in Pennsylvania, Gerald sums it up: "They first need to know their own needs are cared for, then they can learn the other truth of the gospel: 'love your neighbor.'"

Second, the pastor cannot just announce that outreach is important or a command of God. She or he needs to lead the way. As a new sense of joyful worship and warmth are being kindled, the pastor needs to engage in personal outreach and evangelism, most naturally to those who constitute the "extended family" of the members.

Shortly after arriving at my own appointment to a smaller church in Arizona, one of the women in the congregation asked if I would call on her husband who never attended. He had the reputation of being a "strange duck." He loved the desert and worked with the Scout program but didn't have much use for preachers and church. I dropped by one Saturday afternoon. No one answered the door. I left a card saying "Sorry I missed you." Later that evening as I was putting some finishing touches on my sermon, the phone rang. I answered, giving my name. The man's voice on the other end simply said, "Are you really?" I was confused by his inquiry and repeated my name asking if he had the right number. He responded, "Are you *really* sorry . . . ," and then added, "that you missed me?" Aha! The weight of the words finally clicked. I hesitatingly replied, "Yes, . . . I think so." He asked, "When are you coming by next? I'll be here." I grew to love Ben as one of my dearest friends, and he grew to love the Lord and the church. Pastors who visit, reach out, and invite open the door outward and lead the way for the congregation to follow.

Third, stimulate the imagination of individuals and the entire congregation by asking good questions about outreach such as: "When was the last time you invited someone to church? Who are the people around us here who are not involved in a church? Why do you suppose they don't attend? What difference would it make in our community if this church were overflowing with people week after week? What are the problems in the community that need to be addressed? Could we do something about them? What do you really think Jesus had in mind when he told us, 'You will be my witnesses'?"

Fourth, share the stories of other churches that have struggled back from defeat to new life and hope and effective ministry and growth. If this is done too soon, it only frustrates people with a feeling that they are being compared to others, and they are failures or less valuable than those "other" churches who happened to have different situations and weren't facing the same kinds of problems. But enough stories shared at the right time, with the right people, will stimulate ideas about what could happen here. Another possibility often cited as tremendously helpful is taking your leaders to meet with other smaller congregations that have already gone through a turnaround, or inviting members from these congregations to come visit with your people and tell their story, followed by a time of questions and answers.

Fifth, a little success in seeing new faces and the return of old familiar faces long absent goes a long way to change the attitude of evangelistic outreach. Likewise, the sense of having made a real difference in the lives of others through a caring ministry reminds everyone that serving in love is its own blessing. A Salvation Army Captain in North Dakota shared: "As new people began coming, our people lowered their defenses, and their attitude changed to one of acceptance. This generated a new excitement within the congregation. Suddenly the members became proud and jumped on the bandwagon."

Sixth, the best energy and concern for outreach comes simply because people recognize themselves as blessed. In God's divine providence, when the Spirit of God has wrought "a new creation" and "everything has become new" (2 Corinthians 5:17), the people of God are led as was Paul to discover they are "ambassadors for Christ" (5:20). A second-career pastor in Georgia who served a multidenominational four-point charge, wrote:

> Members here have established a new commitment to outreach and mission. As pastor here over the last few years, I have seen the church go from being very conservative in the outreach area to being very liberal. They were contented, or maybe complacent is a better word, with things as they were. At the beginning of my tenure here, we set some specific goals to expand our facilities. This activity and involvement seemed to lift the passivity from this congregation and when this project was completed, new ideas came forth on the best way to use these

facilities in meeting the needs of the local community. New commit-
tees were formed and more outreach ministries were started. The pas-
sive stance of the congregation was changed into an active one and a
sense of progress surfaced and we all celebrated a victory.

4. Expanding the Financial Base

In the outreach described above, the church began to discover how to reach out after its own facilities were upgraded and expanded. Some writers and prophetic voices today are opposed to spending any more money on buildings. This isn't a new idea. The hermits of ancient days decided the best way to find spiritual renewal was to abandon all claim to any material attachments and live in the simplest of conditions. This ascetic lifestyle was seen as more faithful to Jesus who himself had "nowhere to lay his head" (Matthew 8:20) and who seemed to speak against building larger barns to store the harvest (Luke 12:13-21). But these naysayers and misinterpreters of the texts neglect to notice that Jesus accepted invitations to even the nicest of homes, regularly attended synagogue, and visited the Temple for worship, and counseled against storing up treasures for ourselves but not against spending money—especially for the business of the kingdom: "For where your treasure is, there your heart will be also" (Luke 12:34).

Pastors of small churches frequently report inadequate finances and poor stewardship are a constant problem, and the facilities are poorly maintained and inadequate. Therefore, one of the most practical and important problems tackled by successful pastors is to find and free the money needed to upgrade the church facilities and instill a new sense of pride and power for ministry. There may be no easier way initially to enlist both finances and effort, especially from men in the congregation, than through a program to enhance the structures owned by the church. If the vision of what is possible has begun to be instilled in the people and the first signs of new life and new members have been recognized, it is time to invest in the future. Six strategies to leap the "finances and facilities" obstacle emerge from the experiences of our turnaround pastors.

First, don't make the mistake of assuming there is no money, either already available but hidden, or potentially in the families supporting the church. Multiple stories were told concerning pastors discovering major funds unknown to most members of the church. Treasurers and other financial officers who have served the church over many years are frequently quite conservative about spending money and may have a strong sense of being the guardians of church funds against the "unnecessary" projects recommended by the parade of new pastors or "those denominational people." Their interest in protecting the church's monies may, in time, become its own special form of ownership and control.

One pastor discovered $72,000 in certificates of deposit not on the records and thus hidden "safely" from the denomination. Another pastor reported finding—through intentional and resented "snooping" in things that "were none of his business"—$12,000 in an account marked "building fund." At the time he was a college student living with his family in a four hundred-square-foot "parsonage" and trying to remind the little church meeting in their old, open-country, white-frame chapel that they needed to provide better if they were ever going to attract a regular pastor. They had been through three pastors in the six months before he naively accepted the invitation. He stayed for thirteen years through many dangers, toils, and snares. He finished college and seminary and helped the church become a fully functioning, revitalized congregation. There were eighteen resident members, and twelve were in worship the first Sunday he arrived. When he left, the church had built one new parsonage and was considering purchasing another, it had bought land and built a new sanctuary and education facility, it was holding two services and averaging over 200 in attendance, and its annual budget was $150,000. Don't assume there isn't any money; look for it and ask for it, and invest in the kingdom.

Second, no matter how difficult for the pastor's family to make ends meet on the salary provided, it is critically important to model financial stewardship—even sacrificial giving and tithing—if it is going to be taught or preached to the members. Some pastors avoid the subject entirely and simply say, "I leave that to the laypeople." This is a mistake. Giving is a spiritual discipline and needs to be addressed as such by the spiritual leader. David Heetland, vice president for development at Garrett-Evangelical Theological Seminary, believes the greatest financial problem in our churches is the lack of a clear theology of stewardship among the ministers. He writes:

> The church has barely tapped its full financial potential—largely because people in the church have not been adequately informed, inspired, or invited to give. Some sobering research has been done by empty tomb, inc., suggesting that while the incomes of church members are rising, the percentage given to the church is declining. I believe ministers must face the fact that they have played a role in this decline by abdicating their role as strong leaders in financial stewardship.[6]

When the time comes to talk about stewardship for the sake of realizing dreams and recovering a sense of vitality for the future, what leaders do—both clergy and lay—speaks much louder than what they say. In reality, stewardship, like faith, is more caught than taught!

There is no need to tell anyone how much to give, but there is a need to tell why to give and how to make stewardship decisions. When the pastor leads in this matter as a sign of deep commitment to Christ and his church in *this* place, it says *we* are going to make it, and the Lord will provide.

It is discouraging to know that some pastors communicate by announcement or simply by lack of regular and sacrificial giving that they believe their "tithe" is contained in having to work for such small remuneration. No church can be led to true stewardship by one who refuses to practice it. This is itself a form of boycott and anger, neither of which work well to renew a congregation in grace and accomplish the miracles that seem beyond reach. One pastor reported that during his second year the parsonage had been broken into, he had received death threats, and in other subtle ways was told to move. He stuck it out because he knew he was called to that church. After the sixth year, he went one morning to get in his twenty-year-old Volkswagen with 200,000 miles on it and found an envelope in the front seat containing 160 hundred dollar bills and a short note that read "new car." Faithful and sacrificial stewardship begets faithful and sacrificial stewardship.

Third, remember that the initial goal is to change the sense of congregational pride or self-esteem. One simple formula included:

> Step one was to cause the people to take pride in the appearance of their church building—new sidewalks, wheelchair ramp, fellowship hall renovated, grass neatly mowed and trimmed weekly. Bulletin boards are changed regularly, . . . the church now has the appearance that something is going on here.

There may be more important projects needing to be done, but first work together to give a fresh face to what is already constructed or add that relatively inexpensive change that will say to insiders and outsiders alike, "We're on the move." One student pastor in upstate New Jersey started with something as simple as planting flowers. When they bloomed, she took a picture of all the members standing at the front of the chapel behind the flowers. The photo was distributed to everyone, and this simple "renovation project" bore wonderful fruit and instilled a new sense of pride and welcome.

Anyone who has lived in a home for more that six months no longer sees the tarnish, cracks, and unfinished projects the way visitors do. Our home had a half-painted bathroom door that was almost never noticed or mentioned until we began to think of putting the house up for sale. New people will more likely feel welcomed as visitors if the church buildings and facilities are "attractive." Think about the meaning of that word.

Fourth, focus on financial stewardship as a spiritual discipline and not primarily a way to raise money or pay bills. Small churches, like families, are much more oriented toward paying the bills than they are toward long-range financial planning for the future. To shift from bill paying to planned giving and effective stewardship involves a shift in values that will come as dreams and visions are linked to spiritual renewal. Money is a gift of God to be invested for the glory of God in accomplishing the things of God.

One pastor reported that as lives were being spiritually refreshed, and as the church tried to do something significant in the community, the end-of-the-month financial statement went from showing what wasn't paid to having a regular surplus of $1,200. A woman in the church told me boldly:

> *One of the most important factors contributing to our growth was we learned how to spend money. Our women's group was reminded by one of our members, "You don't get money if you don't spend money." Before, we never had any money and people were always complaining. Now, because we've decided there are so many things needing to be done, we're raising and spending ten times what we used to and now no one complains. We're really enjoying it!*

Fifth, be creative and imaginative in both stewardship education and in raising money. It ought to be fun, as well as rewarding, to give. Small churches benefit enormously from the fellowship that accompanies special fund-raising projects that are aimed at something significant. A second career pastor from West Virginia described how her small church learned regular giving but also enjoyed other opportunities for raising money, such as:

> *fund-raisers such as the fall bazaar, selling Easter candy, bake sales, white elephant sales, and special collections for the needy whenever necessary. An "Outreach Jar" is used each month for a different cause such as the improvement fund, for a family burned out of their home, for two children who were burned, and for hunger.*

Sixth, affirm the efforts made, and continue to pray for and expect great things, and they will come. A pastor in Michigan shared this quote from one of the church's lifelong members: "For a small church we carry a pretty heavy financial burden, but we're a six-lane church when it comes to giving." For a church to know it is a six-lane church, and to act like a "six-lane church in a one-horse town," requires at least one bold voice to create the momentum and the motto.

Saying "thank you" for every job well done is especially important in smaller fellowships. There are always subtle dangers connected with our giving. We do it for many reasons, not all of them are as spiritual as others. But joyful gratitude is an appropriate response to almost every gift offered in Jesus' name and for his work. It usually takes four to six years for complete turnaround to come in most churches. Giving is not only linked to spiritual renewal and vision but also to trust. Trust takes time. But pastors who have learned to say how much they appreciate the efforts of their people are laying a foundation that will stand the times of trial and the test of storms. Persons in any family need to hear that someone is proud of them.

5. Handling Snakes and Other Conflicts

Here in Kentucky it is not unusual to read occasionally about someone in the mountains being bitten by a poisonous snake during a worship service. In fact, I have provided the opportunity for seminary students to visit these churches as part of their cross-cultural exposure and as an introduction to folk religions. These images came to mind when I heard a pastor in Florida recount the following experience: A woman who had been visiting his church told a friend at work where she had been attending worship. Her friend immediately showed agitation and warned her to not go back to that church because she had heard that it was one of those "snake-handling churches." The woman was surprised but called the pastor to set the record straight. Indeed, as it turned out, a newly hired custodian had spread this story after overhearing a conversation in the sanctuary between the minister's wife and a sound systems consultant. The consultant clearly did say they would need a "snake" (in audio language, a large bundle of cables bound together to keep individual wires from having to be taped down or run separately). The pastor's wife asked how big a snake it would have to be. The consultant answered, "I can't say for sure, but a big one."

All snakes don't look alike or bite the same way, but when the heat gets turned up in the middle of changes, we ought to be ready for whatever might come out of the fire (Acts 28:3-6). The "snakes" most likely to emerge in times of change when the fires of the Spirit are beginning to blaze are those involving power struggles and interpersonal conflict.

Handling these snakes of conflict, like handling anything dangerous, requires courage, faith, gentleness, and skill. This skill has to do with gifts and graces, as well as training. Some will naturally be better at it than others. But all who hope to be turnaround leaders might as well face the reality that they will have plenty of opportunity to learn by experience if by no other method.

General conflict management theory[7] describes several options for how persons respond to conflict. Norman Shawchuck and Robert Moeller described these in an article titled "Animal Instincts: Five Ways Church Members Will React in a Fight."[8]

> We all develop survival responses in threatening situations. Corporate psychologists have labeled these responses with animal names (for the solutions they seek): sharks ("I win; you lose"), foxes ("Everyone wins a little and loses a little"), turtles ("I withdraw"), teddy bears ("I'll lose so you can win"), and owls ("Let's find a way for everyone to win").

The value of identifying these five creatures is not only to show how different members react but also to recognize and evaluate our own approaches to handling conflict.

Some of us, especially the relational types who like small churches because they value relationships highly, tend to function like turtles, teddy bears, or foxes. We handle conflict by avoidance, submission, or egalitarian compromise. The first approach will never produce a leader for change. Change produces conflict. To avoid conflict is to abdicate leadership. Pastors can function this way and be loved, but they cannot lead a church out of trouble. The second approach sounds most "Christian" to some ears, and passages like "blessed are the peacemakers" (Matthew 5:9) and "Do nothing from selfish ambition or conceit, but in humility regard others as better than yourselves" (the self-emptying "kenosis" passage from Philippians 2:3-11) come to mind. But teddy bears will always be eaten by sharks. And there is a danger in giving too much away to sharks. Shawchuck and Moeller write: "When 'I must win' individuals are allowed to rule the church, anger builds in others, people feel coerced, and a dangerous dependency on the strong-willed individual develops."[9] This is true whether the shark is a member or a pastor.

The compromise suggested by foxes solves all problems in the same way: "Divide the living boy in two; then give half to the one, and half to the other" (1 Kings 3:25). Solomon's wisdom and the woman who truly loved the child saw through the folly of such a mechanical and egalitarian approach to equality. Such an approach may work well in some situations, but it can also destroy the dynamic and responsive life of the church as Christ's body, which does not exist simply to make everyone happy but to serve the purposes of the risen Lord.

The recommended approach is that of the collaborative owl. The authors write, "Collaborators see disputes as an opportunity to strengthen a group, not destroy it."[10] They describe three important tasks necessary for wise owls to handle conflict as collaborators ("co-labor"ers). First, generate as much useful information as possible about all sides of the issue. Second, help the group see where they agree, not just where they don't. And third, bring all who are involved into the decision-making process and motivate them to personally commit themselves to the final agreement. This is indeed hard work. In fact, it can't always be the approach to every conflict. Sometimes it is best to withdraw. (Does it really matter if the memorial table is in the "right" place?) Sometimes it is necessary to be a shark and say, "Here I stand! I can do nothing else. God help me! Amen."[11] But when it comes time for the church to turn the corner for its future, only the owl can solve conflict in a way that leads to life and health and peace.

Some issues, and even some persons, need to be confronted head-on. Other issues need to be waited out, while others need to be waded through. Pray for wisdom to know the difference. Be careful, but don't be afraid of the snakes. Sometimes, as the consultant recommended to the church in Florida, a congregation needs a good "snake" to let the new song be heard loud and clear by everyone. Handle the snakes when necessary, but do it, as our Appalachian friends remind us, in the Spirit and in faith. Above all, don't pretend they aren't present or dangerous. But keep loving and keep leading. That is the meaning of God's call to leadership.

Fresh Fish

John from Kansas shared this fable:

I once heard the story of a fisherman who had a secret for preserving fish in the days before refrigeration. Everyone back then kept their fish alive in deep wells in the ships. But his fish were always firm and fresh and better than the others. He consistently got a better market price than his competitors, and they longed to know his secret. After his death his fellow fishermen went on board his ship to search for the secret. They discovered an enormous flathead catfish in the well. Though he ate a few of the fish dumped in, the real benefit of his presence was that he kept all the other fish moving, stirred up, and on the alert. If you will, he kept them "fresh."

John explained the images, but perhaps they are best left, as are most parables, to be discovered. We move next to some reflections on fishing for people.

Questions for Discussion

• Which three of the "obstacles" or "factors impeding revitalization" have been most challenging for your people? Why?

• Read through the J. B. Phillips translation of 1 Thessalonians 1:1-5 again (p. 64) and the questions that follow. Which question seems most important to you? Why?

• Harold Percy also asks probing questions (pp. 66-67) that help clarify a congregation's mission and vision for the future. Explore your answers to these questions with others and try to discern where you have the greatest agreement or disagreement.

• One of the common qualities noted in turnaround churches that helped them become more invested in outreach was a sense of being "blessed." What are the blessings of God you would list for your church?

- Conflict and various kinds of "snakes" appear in every congregation. Name one you have experienced. How well was it handled? How could such challenges be better handled in the future?

CHAPTER 5

Turning toward Others

Do not fear, or be afraid; have I not told you from of old and declared it? You are my witnesses! Is there any god besides me? There is no other rock; I know not one. —Isaiah 44:8

Small-church approaches to evangelism need to be person centered. This is the pattern and strength of the small church. Super churches attract people through their winsome pulpiteer and their glamorous programs. The small church attracts through the contacts people have with its members.[1]

Evangelism—Whose Task?

It would be difficult to read the Bible and not recognize God's desire to seek and to save humanity. This is accomplished through God's redemptive acts in history, and ultimately through Jesus Christ, the Savior of the world. God's people are sent to be witnesses to and heralds of this wonderful news. In fact, it might be said that one reason God "comes" to us for our own salvation is to "send" us on a mission to be instruments of divine grace in the lives of others.

Moses heard this clearly when God came to him and spoke from the burning bush, saying, "I have observed the misery of my people who are in Egypt; I have heard their cry. . . . So come,

I will send you to Pharaoh to bring my people, the Israelites, out of Egypt" (Exodus 3:7, 10). Isaiah heard the call that day in the temple when the voice said, "Whom shall I send, and who will go for us?" and he responded "Here am I; send me!" (Isaiah 6:8). And part of Isaiah's message is to remind God's people they are all to be bearers of the light and the gospel. "I am the LORD, I have called you in righteousness, I have taken you by the hand and kept you; I have given you as a covenant to the people, a light to the nations" (Isaiah 42:6). Likewise, the words of Jesus clearly remind us that we are sent as he was sent (John 20:21) and we are his witnesses to all (Matthew 5:13-16; Acts 1:8).

Although it is difficult not to see this emphasis in the Scripture, it appears quite easy for individuals and congregations to ignore or abdicate this responsibility and assign it by default, if not overtly, to someone else. In most churches, the person seen as responsible for the witness and evangelism work of the church is the pastor. One reason for this is the interesting way the Greek word for "evangelize" has been translated for centuries in many English versions of the New Testament.

The Problem of Translation

For example, Philip (selected in Acts 6:5 by the early church to care for the needs of neglected widows) is later called "the evangelist" (Acts 21:8). The only activities of Philip we are able to read about related to his evangelism are described in Acts 8, where all *but* the apostles are scattered from Jerusalem because of persecution (8:1). Philip, and the other "regular" Christians, led of the Holy Spirit, simply went about "evangelizing" (Acts 8:4, 12, 35). Read these passages in almost every English translation and discover that "to evangelize" is constantly translated "to preach" or "to proclaim" the gospel. Even when Philip climbs up into the chariot of the Ethiopian official to have a marvelous one-on-one conversation with him about Jesus, he "preaches" or "proclaims" it, according to most of our traditional translations.

When the average Christian or church member today hears the words "preach the gospel," he or she hears only "preach" and says, "OK, it must be your job, preacher!" Even if smaller churches refer to their clergy as "pastor" or "minister" instead of "preacher," nothing is gained. The problem is that evangelism, often along with much other ministry, seems to have been clearly labeled by the Holy Bible itself as something accomplished by a single means called preaching and a special person ("parson") called the preacher. Thus, those not called to be preachers believe they have every good reason to be off the hook when it comes to evangelism. Such thinking may be largely subconscious, but it may be at least one of the reasons why it is often difficult to get persons to sign up for training in evangelism or even to think about this being a whole congregation's task. The image communicated is to preach at persons, and most of us intuitively know the best place for this to happen is in church and from the pulpit.[2]

The Problem of Transmission

One of the tragedies in many churches today, especially in mainline churches, is that no one is very involved in evangelism.[3] Although almost all congregations have a preacher, most preachers see themselves as shepherds of the flock and program managers—not evangelists. In many cases, these pastors have received little seminary training or encouragement to be involved in evangelism. Whatever preaching or teaching they engage in is designed much more to instruct and challenge the faithful than to engage and invite a turnaround for "the perishing," "the dying," "the erring," "the fallen," and "tell them of Jesus, the mighty to save."

One painful image of what could happen in some churches, even the so-called successful ones, might be found in this Associated Press newspaper article that appeared several years ago.

> NEW ORLEANS—Although 100 lifeguards were present, a fully clothed man drowned at a party to celebrate the first summer in memory without a drowning at a New Orleans city pool.
>
> Jerome Moody . . . was a guest at the party. . . . Four lifeguards were on duty at the party and more than half the 200 people there were certified lifeguards.
>
> It was not known when Moody got in the water or how he drowned.

They pulled him out and tried to revive him until emergency medical attendants arrived. An autopsy confirmed that he had drowned.

The goal for churches, as well as other life-protecting and life-saving institutions, is never merely to have certified personnel on hand or to celebrate a glorious history. People in the life-saving business must always be alert to danger, aware of and sensitive to every person within their purview, and engaged in their primary work without distraction. Otherwise, a glorious history can become an ironic mockery worn like a millstone around the neck.

Getting Focused for Outreach

In the last chapter we explored the recommendations of turn-around pastors for keeping a congregation on the right path—facing the giants, overcoming the obstacles, and surviving the dangers and snares. Strange as it may seem (and it usually does seem strange to smaller churches), now our objective is to discover how to encourage church members to risk moving off the path in order that others might find "the Way." To set the stage, it may be helpful to see what turnaround pastors answered when asked, "What has contributed most to the growth of this congregation?" Their top twenty answers ranked by frequency of occurrence follow.

Growth Factors in Smaller Churches

1. An atmosphere of love and acceptance
2. Pastoral initiative
3. New programs and outreach ministries
4. Alive, open, inviting worship
5. An attitude of faith and grace
6. A strong Bible focus
7. An emphasis on children and youth
8. Hard work and a desire to grow
9. Inviting friends to church
10. An evangelism emphasis
11. Prayer

12. Emphasis on gifts and discipleship
13. Laypersons involved in visitation
14. Laypersons involved in ministry
15. The blessing of God's Holy Spirit
16. The church location and a growing community
17. Special outreach and evangelistic events
18. Using a strategic planning process
19. Using new people in leadership
20. A pastor willing to stay

It is easy to see by looking at this list that pastors serving smaller churches effective in outreach, evangelism, and growth have a very balanced view of ministry. They are not *narrowly* focused on evangelism. The primary credit for growth is not assigned to a visitation program, even though when asked what they would change if they could in the church's outreach efforts, these pastors indicated "more lay visitation" as their second most-often expressed wish. But notice that growth producing outreach and evangelism in small churches is primarily related to inviting persons to attend warm and exciting experiences of worship (items 1, 4, 5, and 6).

A second cluster of growth factors emerges around new programs and ministries that have an intentional outreach and evangelistic dimension (items 3, 7, and 10). Perhaps item 17 could also be included in this category. But it is clear that evangelism and outreach leading to growth in these churches are not primarily periodic special events. Evangelism that leads to growth is an ongoing effort to contact and invite persons in the community to join with the pastor and members of the church as together they seek God's blessing and love, and to accept one another, pay attention to God's Word, and witness to the good news of Christ.

One additional group of factors could be collected around the theme of giving new persons a place in the family. Notice especially items 12, 13, 14, and 19. These factors describe a church where laypersons, including newcomers, are being trained and equipped to discover the joy of reaching out to others and giving leadership to the congregation. Together these growth ingredients contribute to a sense of excitement, momentum, and fulfillment for those who have already been reached and who are now identifying themselves as growing disciples of Jesus Christ. I will speak more about this in the next chapter, but it should be noted that growth is dependent not only on evangelism defined as reaching out or converting but also as discipling and developing.

Growth Stages in Smaller Churches

When asked to identify the steps or stages their congregations went through on their way to new life and growth, turnaround pastors indicate they often had to begin with "healing the past" and then move on to "catching the vision" and "finding successful ways to reach new people." Several pastors included a list of five to ten items representing a clear step-by-step approach to renewal and outreach.

> *Our stages were: (1) confusion and bickering, (2) power struggle, (3) frustration, (4) a time of decision to be the church instead of a small group of people playing church, (5) adjustment, (6) growth began with new people coming into the church as well as old members coming back, (7) increased vision and outreach.*

Another described the process as working hard with a spouse to reach out to others until the new people coming helped force the changes.

> *We visited. We listened. We acted on people's suggestions. The stages we went through were: (1) My wife started a children's program which reached 47 as we adopted the lessons learned by listening. We were not pushy, but consistently witnessing and present. (2) The children brought their parents. (3) The parents expressed their needs and desires. (4) We realized we needed them as much as they needed us. (5) We started programs to reach out. (6) We received visitors warmly. (7) Once they joined we gave them a job to do. (8) We received them into the "inner sanctum" of the church.*

For one pastor, starting over was exactly that. "We closed down the church for nine months and began a Bible study group with new people."

The key ingredient, either before or after healing the wounds and catching the new vision, is the actual experience of success at reaching new people. New faces and families in church enable members to believe again in a brighter future and invest again in their buildings, their witness, and their efforts to please God. When the seventy returned from the mission Jesus sent them on, they "returned with joy" because they had sensed a new power to be effective in Jesus' name (Luke 10:17). Once the twelve or the seventy in smaller churches today experience a similar success in reaching out in Jesus' name, they too find a new joy and momentum for ministry.

Efforts to Contact New People

When the turnaround pastors were asked to identify their intentional efforts to contact and reach new people, their top fifteen answers were:

1. Emphasize inviting a friend
2. Utilize the phone, letters, ads, signs
3. Start new programs
4. Welcome visitors
5. Encourage lay visitation
6. Follow up with visitors
7. Conduct pastoral visitation
8. Focus on children's ministries
9. Deliver welcome packets and baked goods
10. Offer pastoral care to the community
11. Redirect existing programs outward
12. Clarify the meaning of being Christian
13. Pray intentionally for unreached people
14. Provide opportunities for new people to serve
15. Plan for special evangelistic events

In and of itself this is a significant collection of outreach strategies for smaller churches. But when the answers to all three outreach and growth questions (growth factors, growth stages, and intentional efforts) are combined with what is known about the pastors themselves, the results are very clear. Successful results in outreach, evangelism, and church growth in smaller churches depend on: (1) having a pastor who leads in evangelism, (2) training, planning, and goal setting for growth, (3) inviting friends and family to church, (4) designing programs to reach new people, (5) visiting all prospects, (6) enhancing the church's image through promotion and advertising, (7) holding special evangelistic events, (8) clarifying the meaning of being Christian, (9) praying for God to touch people's lives, and (10) using the gifts of all for the work of the kingdom. The rest of this chapter is dedicated to exploring in more detail the first five items mentioned in the above formula, along with a few observations on the other items thrown in for good measure.

Reaching New People

While I was sitting at my computer working on a manuscript, my youngest son approached me to ask if I would help him with homework. Like his father, and perhaps others, he had a tendency to put off as long as possible the most challenging assignments. So, twice in one week, late at night, he asked if I would type for him as he composed an "original story." He talked, I typed. During the sometimes slow and labored process, I wasn't sure if either story was ever going to "arrive." Nevertheless, as the creative juices flowed and special twists were added to each, I began to see a gift I had never noticed before. The stories were actually quite good, perhaps even brilliant—from a proud father's perspective, of course—and I told him so.

How do we get started in anything that may be a challenge but could also be part of God's provision for a fuller and more fruitful life? Usually we need both a push and a pull. When Jesus sent out the disciples to carry the gospel of the kingdom to others, they were given an assignment. They were pushed as though by a mother bird who knew the time had come for them to leave the nest. When we read God's design for us to be witnesses, or hear the words of Jesus describing believers as salt and light, don't we feel the push? Isn't the Great Commission a push, an assignment, a command? Yet both Jesus and Paul describe the work of the Holy Spirit as an inward longing, a pull toward doing the will of the Father, a love that controls us.

1. Push and Pull Pastors

Which of us would get moving without the outward push? Which of us would keep moving without the upward pull? The greatest, most powerful and creative story ever released won't be written in the lives of others who have never heard it unless we take it and tell it. But frightened fledglings like ourselves will not get on with it unless we have to and then discover we want to. Pastors who understand this dynamic tension and bring to their congregations both the push and the pull of doing God's will and offering Christ to others succeed in bringing new life not only to their congregations but also to their communities.

As noted earlier, nearly 90 percent of these pastors remember a definite conversion experience of their own and are in pastoral ministry in large part because they want others to know God and find eternal life. They are motivated both by the pull of God's love and the possibility of changed lives, as well as by the push of obedience to Christ's commands.[4]

Regardless of the motivation, evangelism is central to the work of turnaround pastors. Richard, from Maryland, boldly announced, "I feel all pastors are called to evangelism, and secondly to church growth." Bob wrote from Alabama, "Evangelism is to the church what wet is to water, you can't have one without the other. Evangelism is the church, the church is evangelism." Duane offered this helpful definition:

> *Evangelism must be understood as a natural thing to do, and not something that is a program of the church. Sharing your faith (or lack of it) is what we do every day without realizing it. Evangelism is simply doing it intentionally in an unobtrusive way. Making people aware of what Jesus has done for them, helps them to share that with others.*

And David, a pastor in Florida, asserted, "A biblical, Christ-centered church should be involved in growth. Evangelism should be incorporated in all aspects of the church life."

Their approaches to evangelism vary considerably, but most are involved in their own efforts at evangelizing as well as trying to get their congregations involved. John, who was thirty-eight before he entered pastoral ministry, said, "I've been telling others about my conversion almost daily since then." Even though many wished they had more training in personal evangelism, it was frequently suggested that there was no better way to help others come to faith in Christ than face-to-face. Others described their approach more in terms of pastoral involvement in the community such as doing weddings and funerals for unchurched couples and families. Still others spoke in terms of preaching and teaching with ample opportunity for people to consider Christ's claims and respond to his invitation either in public worship or in opportunities offered for more private conversations.

These pastors have a deep commitment to both personal witness and to ministries of evangelism; and wherever they serve, they are going to exercise both the push and the pull approaches to bring their congregations along with them as they reach out to others needing to hear about Christ and belong to his faith community. Their sense of urgency and their personal efforts are contagious. They use whatever seems most appropriate and keep at it until it works. Eric from Alabama described this attitude and investment as follows:

> Too many congregations and pastors get the idea that because a community is not growing rapidly, they cannot grow. They give up on their lost neighbors. Last year, a sixty-year-old man was saved, baptized, and united with the church. He had lived in this community most of his life and was not considered "reachable." We can never give up praying, witnessing, and sharing God's love through every means available to win all we can to Jesus Christ. Our church has not forgotten that.

2. Training, Planning, and Goal Setting

Pastors committed to fruitful turnaround provide for some kind of training, planning, and goal setting for church growth. Some organize an evangelism or outreach and mission committee. This team of four to six committed persons meets to discuss their concerns, their dreams, their ideas, and their frustrations. Sometimes they go together to training events held elsewhere, and return home and thoroughly discuss what they heard to determine what seems most appropriate for their circumstances.

On occasion, they have an outside speaker or consultant from the denomination or other resource center come meet with them to get them started and encourage their progress. Frequently the pastors themselves have access to materials and a storehouse of ideas, and lead their teams through quite a variety of training experiences. These range from witnessing and preparation for visiting, to full-blown long-range planning and goal setting that is infused with a yearning to reach lost persons.

Robert from Georgia described his church's efforts to reach out, saying, "We have classes on witnessing, teaching, and receiving." He trained people to talk about their faith, to lead classes and Bible studies, and to know how to make visitors and newcomers feel warmly welcomed. He added, "Our people go to seminars elsewhere for training and inspiration. I am training the people to function without a pastor, if necessary. If they are going to survive as a church, they must do the work of the church and not leave it to the pastor." Later we will discuss just how critical this observation is when it comes to the *beyond* of turnaround. Even smaller congregations that experience renewal under the leadership like that described in these pages struggle with keeping their momentum during pastoral transitions unless they are learning to "do the work of the church and not leave it to the pastor."

But sometimes even the most elaborate training efforts seem to be misdirected and ineffective. As some have noted before, shepherds lead their sheep; they don't drive them. One pastor confessed, "All *my* efforts to organize evangelism teams seemed to fizzle, but *they* were already doing the sorts of things needful for effective evangelism. On their own they were inviting and visiting, and they were excited about the church." Training and organizing need to be correlated to what the congregation recognizes as an opportunity or a need and what it accepts as its own way of doing things. Otherwise, the attitude is "If it ain't broke, don't fix it."

What is least complicated and most natural to the understanding of the members will probably garner the most energy and produce the best results. Long-range planning and goal setting have not always fit this description in smaller churches. But several pastors reported significant success with such efforts. Linda, a pastor in Connecticut, held an evangelism workshop with her team of six people, using a denominational planning handbook for evangelism ministries. She reported:

> Before we began we discussed what we wanted to see happen with this workshop. First, we wanted to feel comfortable evangelizing. Second, more than just going through the exercises of the handbook, we committed ourselves to doing something about it when we were finished. In light of the church's problem of not growing, and in light of our mission to share and spread the good news with our community and world, we feel that it is extremely important for us, all of us, to act upon what we have learned.

They examined their strengths, sought out community needs, and recommended to the congregation five specific steps to be taken to better share God's good news through Christ. Once people were clear about what needed to be done, they were ready to give it their very best.

Sometimes the planning began with analysis. Sometimes it began with dreaming. Sometimes it began with setting goals. The most common goal-setting approach was to target a specific percentage of increase in worship attendance or membership, or both. Among those who reported such percentage goals, the most common figure was 10 percent growth over the next year. This was an interesting figure, since the data on the turnaround churches in the study indicated an average membership increase of 56 percent over a five-year period and a 79 percent increase over the same period in worship attendance. Thus, a 10 percent growth goal might be well be within reach of most smaller churches.

It appears that setting such goals, planning to reach them, organizing human energy, and training persons in various skills related to evangelism and outreach are important ingredients in effectively reaching out to others and helping smaller churches grow. But the most important single ingredient in a small church's plan for evangelistic effectiveness, according to the pastors surveyed, still centers around what people do most naturally when they are excited about what God is doing in their lives: they invite people to church.

3. Inviting Friends and Family

Using our natural social networks to reach new people has long been recognized as the most productive method of church growth. Writers in the field have indicated from previous research that larger churches and churches in suburban and urban areas grow most readily through using the friendship network. Churches in smaller towns and rural settings, and smaller churches in general, have grown more through drawing on family contacts. By a greater than two-to-one ratio, persons answered, "Why did you first attend church here?" with "I was invited by a family member." The second most frequent response was "I was invited by a friend or acquaintance." In third place was "I was looking for a new church," and the fourth most common answer was "They offered a program that met my needs."

Growing smaller churches primarily use an attraction approach to evangelism. When they get together, they sense that this is exactly what other people need too, and they become intentional about inviting family members, friends, and neighbors to come to church with them. The best invitations are extended in person—thus the meaning of using the network of "family and friends." But a second way these churches extend the invitation includes contact through advertising and various other methods of community-wide promotion. Posters, brochures, direct mailings, newspapers, newsletters, signs, and door-to-door visits were all included. Perhaps surprising to some, targeted advertising ranked second only to the emphasis on inviting friends and family.

Samples of brochures and newsletters from turnaround churches include such helpful items of information as an introduction (name of the church, address, pastor, phone numbers, a motto or brief mission statement, and so on); worship and Sunday school hours; a list of programs including Sunday school classes, any youth or children's activities, Bible studies, Communion, a men's breakfast, a women's fellowship group, gospel sings, and a list of all groups regularly using the church buildings for meetings. And always there was an invitation to come join them. Growing smaller churches are doing everything they can to say to the community, "We're here, we're listening, we care, and we want you."

Probably the most productive invitational approach involved designating special Sundays as "Invitation Sundays" or "Friendship Sundays." Some designated one or two Sundays a year, others one Sunday a month, as the best day to invite visitors. In either case, this allowed for special preparations that could not be made every Sunday, such as including greeters, a fellowship time with coffee and delicious baked goods, name tags, an easy-to-follow bulletin and order of worship, special music, a straightforward yet sensitive message about the gospel, laypersons prepared to assist in the service, a children's time, no requests for operating funds, a brief testimony or mission moment, cards for visitors to fill out, a visiting team ready to make follow-up calls, a quality special program scheduled that night or the next week to which guests could be invited back, and so on.

Charles and Linda entered pastoral ministry together later in life and had great success with this approach at their very first church. The average attendance at this church during the year before they arrived was twenty-one. On their first Sunday, only eighteen were in attendance, and the three youngest were a nine-year-old girl, a four-week-old baby, and the baby's fifty-year-old mother.

After two months of getting their bearings, Charles purchased a Friend Day packet and began to prepare the congregation for inviting friends to church. Eight weeks before the Friend Day Sunday, he announced the program and told people to begin making plans. Next, he formed a committee of a dozen key members. As pastor he wrote to four community leaders and invited them to be his special guests on Friend Day. He informed them that they would be recognized as friends of the community whether they came or not, and that their letters of response would be read to the congregation. Three weeks before the Friend Day, their letters of acceptance were read and Charles announced he already had ten or more attending as his guests. All letters of acceptance were posted on a large bulletin board in the narthex.

The next Sunday, with two weeks to go, the committee was introduced and presented with Friend Day pins. The acceptance notes or letters from their invited guests were read. All members were encouraged by the growing momentum and were challenged: "Join with us and get involved. All guests are acceptable.

Get your friend to sign that he or she will be coming and next week post their notes with ours on the Friend Day board. It's going to be a great day of worship!" It was, and 151 people crowded into the old sanctuary. It was the first time many could remember that the old, faithful members had to select other seats. Thirty-five new prospects were identified for follow-up. Charles reported, "By repeating the same program twice a year for three years (with a wonderful harvest banquet offered in the fall), our church in Albany, Kentucky received fifty new members, thirty-four by baptism, including six teenage boys who joined together on the same Sunday." This church was newly alive and making plans to reach out to even more of their community in Christian love.

Probably few churches that stress inviting friends to worship use this exact model, but variations on this theme are mentioned as the number one method small churches have used to reach out and make new contacts. When these prospects are loved, encouraged, invited back, and offered clear opportunities to make life-changing decisions for Christ, their lives are transformed and so are the churches that invite them.

4. Designing Programs for New People

Developing a sense of mission and a concern for the community often begin when the small church discovers that its buildings can be used for more than Sunday and Wednesday church programs. Occasionally, this new "opening" of the church consists primarily of providing a place for some community organizations to meet. Duane wrote: "Things started to change when we opened the doors to outside organizations such as Boy Scouts, Girl Scouts, AA meetings, a polling place, etc. We became visible." Other churches reported offering space to such groups as the NAACP, the school board, senior citizens groups, ecumenical programs, parenting groups, and occasionally serving as a crisis center in times of community need.

But opening the church facility to the outside can't be the end of the story. Although some churches may settle for being low-rent landlords or even a space-available charity, growing churches take this "service" at least one step further. They get members involved in working with these groups and identifying with the constituents they serve. Duane went on to say: "One thing that is so very obvious is the amount of time each member is willing to give to volunteer service. My wife now checks blood pressure for anyone who wants it checked the second Sunday of every month, and the third Sunday of the month we open the church and have a covered dish dinner."

The programs used by these turnaround churches to reach out to their communities were myriad. Some were programs common to many churches in lots of communities, such as food pantries, ministries to the homeless, crop walks, tutoring, English as Second Language classes, sports programs, day care, mothers day out, Celebrate Recovery[5] and other 12-step groups, sewing classes, community Bible studies, Vacation Bible school, community choirs, and so forth. But many of the churches developed very special programs to address particular needs and to use their gifts in response to God's calling. When these programs were also used as contact points to talk about personal faith and invite people to church, they became important points of entry for new people looking for a place in God's family.

When the Reverend Eduardo arrived to serve a church in Puerto Rico, there were three families attending and $1.45 in the treasury. Pastor Eduardo was a social worker who felt called by God to serve Christ's church. Today that same little congregation has a membership of nearly 300 and over 200 in average attendance at the morning worship service. In the last fifteen years, they have become an international movement of more than 50 churches in six countries, and their greatest challenge is developing leaders to keep up with what the Holy Spirit is allowing them to be part of.

What contributed most to the growth and success of this once-struggling congregation? Eduardo reported that God first blessed primarily through three "ministries" focused toward the community. First, they reached out to senior citizens through two women who offered ambulatory service to five marginalized elders of the community. Eventually, twenty-eight volunteers served over 132 poor senior citizens in the area. They visited them weekly, coordinated their visits with doctors and public agencies, and celebrated holidays and birthdays with them. The second ministry was aimed at children. Twenty-one Extension Bible schools were started in various locations with more than 250 children involved. These children not only studied the Bible but received counsel and support to become better persons and give themselves in service to others. Third was a program they called "The Ministry of Sick Patients." Volunteers gave two mornings a week to visit in the hospitals. They fed and bathed the patients as well as offered them and their families emotional and spiritual support. Pastor Eduardo reported that the deep concern that the congregation grew to have for evangelism, church growth, stewardship, and theological education began as they reached out to love and serve people all around them.

Gil retired from his first career and went to serve an old, downtown Church of God in Pennsylvania late in life. He arrived in a changing community with nothing but a strong will, a creative mind, a deep faith, a supportive spouse, and twenty faithful worshipers. Along with lots of pastoral visitation in the community and exciting new worship services, programs became very important in reaching new people. The most unusual and original was the "Five Fs" program, "Friends for Freedom from Fear," developed by Gil from the Alcoholics Victorious model that emerged out of AA.

In the twelve-page brochure printed for the program, the purpose statement includes:

> *The Five F's is a group formed to help people with any problem whatsoever, whether caused by such things as chemicals, alcohol, just plain selfishness, or what have you. . . . We come together at our meetings to offer support to each other in our fight against our problems, and to accept that support as a part of the healing process. . . . Any person who has a problem, or is related to one who has a problem, is welcome to join us. The only condition for entering the group is that the person is sincere in wanting help.*

In addition to the Five Fs program, the church designed a Wednesday JOY Bible Club for children, and several other programs for men and women. The twenty in worship who were there when Gil first arrived at the church grew to over 120 in two morning worship services. These new persons were primarily reached through creative, compassionate, unique programs addressing the special needs in people's lives.

Although several kinds of programmatic outreach methods become important to smaller turnaround churches, the most frequently mentioned involve children and youth. Again and again pastors wrote: "We started classes for children and youth and targeted young families. There were only 13 children in the church six years ago, and now we average over 60 in Sunday school every week."

To reach the youth and children, the churches used existing programs such as Sunday school and VBS, as well as starting new programs such as Scouts, day care, youth fellowships, and special music and drama groups.

Tremendous personal and social problems still keep many people from the freedom Christ offers because they don't believe the church really cares about them or their problems. Unchurched Americans often believe the church's only product is judgmental morality or perhaps insurance for the life to come. How will people near our churches discover the salvation Christ provides for this life as well the life to come unless we find ways to reach into their worlds instead of waiting for them to come to ours? Churches using programs to reach out are discovering what Jesus meant when he said, "As the Father has sent me, so I send you" (John 20:21), "Go therefore and make disciples" (Matthew 28:19), and "Let the little children come to me; do not stop them; for it is to such as these that the kingdom of God belongs" (Mark 10:14).

5. Visiting All the Prospects

Although visiting people in their homes (especially unannounced) is not as popular or well received as it once was, in his introduction to *Growing Plans,* Lyle Schaller writes: "The best single approach still is the old-fashioned system of personal visitation."[6] After describing further his rationale for this strong affirmation, Schaller acknowledges that many churches, nevertheless, find this approach difficult or inappropriate.

Sometimes the pastors themselves are not particularly comfortable with the idea. But more often, members who have lived in the community for many years frequently resist risking their relationships with neighbors and acquaintances through what they perceive to be an unnatural "intrusion" approach to witnessing.

On the other hand, many pastors and congregations have had exciting results and affirming responses from almost all persons contacted. Perhaps much of the difference is in attitude and people skills as well as how the effort is modeled and communicated. One way not to promote a visitation program appeared in the bulletin of a church in Pennsylvania. "The outreach committee has enlisted 25 visitors to make calls on people who are not afflicted with any church." If the typist was subconsciously or otherwise expressing his or her real convictions, the visitation team was in for a rough time of it. Even if people came, why would they want to stay?

Generally, pastors serving the turnaround congregations indicated lay visitation and pastoral visitation were very important methods for contacting new people. For some, especially many of the pastors themselves and sometimes their spouses, this means calling on those identified as inactive or unchurched, as well as visiting in hospitals, nursing homes, and even door-to-door in some communities, just to get acquainted and to extend an invitation to church. Much more commonly, however, visitation programs were described as "people who take cookies (pies, loaves of bread, cakes, flowers off the altar, coffee mugs with the church name, and so on) to the visitors," and "a follow-up phone call by one of our members before Thursday." One pastor who recognized the fruit of his own visiting commented, "We need more people to: (1) do follow-up visits to visitors, (2) visit the sick and shut-ins, (3) visit members on key days (death in family, birthday, anniversary), and (4) visit new families in area."

One very encouraging story of expanding the visitation team was shared about a Church of the Brethren congregation in rural Pennsylvania:

> The Steven's Hill Church had struggled for years. I wasn't around in those days, but they say that the constant bickering between two families had prevented the church from growing. Two and a half years ago the decision was made to close the doors.
>
> A man named Bill felt called of the Lord to reopen the church. Bill was a 61-year-old sheep farmer who had served as an evangelist and an interim pastor in several churches over the years. With the blessings of the district, Bill began visiting in the community and started a Bible study with some of the remnant of the congregation and

several new people. He recruited another well-grounded couple to assist him in his visitation and by October the Bible study group had grown to more than twenty.

As the story continues, several began to talk about reopening the church. They worked to make improvements on the old building and decided to use an aerial map and visit every home within two miles of the church. The estimate was about 200 homes. In reality there were more than 700. They visited more than 400. An active member described the results as follows:

"A year and a half later our attendance has grown to over 70 on a Sunday morning, 80 percent of whom were not active in a church a year ago. Many of the people in our church are 'baby boomers' who grew up in the church, but stopped attending for various reasons. We have contacted homes as many as ten times before families have come to church the first time. We always fear that we will turn people off with our repeated visits and calls, but that does not seem to be the case. We've found that it's often helpful to have different people visit the same household. That way, before they come to church, they already know several people."

To sum up, we attribute the success of our church to the guidance of the Holy Spirit, persistent visitation, a good Sunday school and nursery, a friendly atmosphere, and sound biblical preaching.

Sometimes success in visitation simply seems to be a matter of getting a willing team together, but many of the pastors themselves admitted they were still adjusting and learning how to make the best evangelistic visits. A few, like Bill, had experience in serving as evangelists, or had been trained in evangelistic programs, or had benefited from working with various evangelistic organizations. But many felt inadequately prepared themselves to know how to engage basic gospel conversations and lead another person to Christ, and thus had little inclination to train laypersons to become more effective visitors and witnesses.

One of the most encouraging stories was shared by Val from Pennsylvania. After finishing his M.Div. degree and pastoring for five years, he said:

I was scared to death that someone might ask me, "How do I become a Christian?" or "What are the basic Christian beliefs?" I was convinced that I could answer most of their questions using theological language from seminary, but I didn't know if I could translate into the

---

language of the average person. I talked with my district superintendent who suggested I go to Ft. Lauderdale and attend an Evangelism Explosion seminar for pastors and use whatever I could. I was actually shocked when for the first time in my life a person said, "Yes, I'd like to make this decision."

Following this training, Val offered a two-hour seminar to some of his members and claims it was a milestone. After moving to another parish, he trained first one and then another to work with him to follow up Sunday visitors every Sunday evening. Soon four people were involved, two visiting with the pastor, and two staying behind at the church to pray. He reported it became a wonderful experience for those on both sides of the task. One very important aspect of their training was the emphasis on learning to tell the gospel using everyday words and not a lot of "church language." They also learned how to use various questions to get deeply into spiritual matters, including: "On a scale of one to ten, how would you rate your life?" and "If you were to meet Jesus today walking down the street, and he asked, 'Why should I accept you?' what would you say?"

This church finally went over the 200 mark in worship for the first time in twenty years, and within two years had received more than fifty new members. When asked how this all happened, one of the key lay leaders said:

> *Much of our success is because of our visitation program. Visitors at worship, new residents, and new children in Sunday school are all visited by Evangelism Teams. Over half of the people we visit come back to our church and eventually join our church family.*

Val reported that few made decisions the first time they were visited or heard the gospel explained in very personal terms that invite a response. But as the months passed and people had additional opportunities to hear this challenge, be loved by the congregation, and feel the tug of the Holy Spirit on their souls, they joyfully responded and became committed members of the church.

These were exciting, growing, revitalized, evangelistic congregations whose members were learning the importance of personal witnessing through visitation programs. Although visitation ministries took many different forms in these churches, there is no question about the benefit of face-to-face contact, conversation, and prayer with people who are seeking to find their way to God and invest their lives in kingdom work.

Offer Them Christ

Much more could be reported about particular programs and approaches used by small churches to reach out to their communities, but in this chapter we have seen the results of pastors and churches who have caught the vision and invested their energies in faithfully reaching out to turn things around in the lives of those who are faltering. Effective Christian witness involves many forms of mission and ministry, but the core of our witness is still that message of salvation and hope that no other organization can offer. The heartbeat of every Christian congregation must be reflected in the words "Offer them Christ" if it can call itself alive and well. One of my own life investments has been to help more Christian disciples learn how to experience the joy of a more productive life of Christian witness.[7] Said another way, I've helped to enable more Christians to do what Peter advised his fellow believers: "But in your hearts set apart Christ as Lord. Always be prepared to give an answer to everyone who asks you to give the reason for the hope that you have. But do this with gentleness and respect" (1 Peter 3:15 NIV).

It may be time in your church for a little prayerful soul-searching as congregations ask themselves, "What are we trying to do for heaven's sake?"

Questions for Discussion

- The word *evangelism* often means quite different things to different people. What comes to mind when you hear the word? At its best, how do you think evangelism should take place?

- In the list of "growth factors" (pp. 84-85), which three would you say are most at work in your church? Which two or three are most in need of attention? How will this best happen?

- An additional list of efforts made to contact new people appeared on p. 87. Check as many as you think are currently being employed in your congregation. If you were to add one or two, what might they be?

- What intentional efforts to plan for outreach and a new future have you previously experienced in this church or another? What was the outcome?

- Read again this chapter's closing paragraph. How would you answer the question "What are we trying to do for heaven's sake?" What congregational efforts at outreach are contributing most to this goal? What changes do you think are called for?

CHAPTER 6

Developing True Disciples

*I pray that, according to the riches of his glory, he
may grant that you may be strengthened in your
inner being with power through his Spirit, and that
Christ may dwell in your hearts through faith, as you
are being rooted and grounded in love . . . that you
may be filled with all the fullness of God.*

—Ephesians 3:16-17, 19

*We are learning and growing together as a commu-
nity of miraculous expectation, utterly dependent on
God, fully gifted by the Holy Spirit, joyously living
Christ's Great Commandment and Great
Commission.*[1]

E ven a once-over, light reading of the New Testament reveals
that the gospel of the kingdom of God is about something
more than mere rescue. The goal is nothing short of complete restoration and a new creation that begins and ends with
agape love. Jesus himself summarizes this transformation in
words often causing problems for theologians and debaters: "Be
perfect, therefore, as your heavenly Father is perfect" (Matthew
5:48). The task of the church, regardless of its size, is to be full of
miraculous expectation and faithful to the work of Christ to the
end that, "rooted and grounded in love," we might live lives

worthy of being called children of God. To the church he founded in Thessalonica, Paul wrote:

> To this end we always pray for you, asking that our God will make you worthy of his call and will fulfill by his power every good resolve and work of faith, so that the name of our Lord Jesus may be glorified in you, and you in him, according to the grace of our God and the Lord Jesus Christ. (2 Thessalonians 1:11-12)

The natural inquiry to follow the emphasis on outreach and evangelism addressed in the last chapter is: "How do the pastors of turnaround churches enable their members to mature in faith, to do the work of faith, to exercise their gifts for ministry, and to become true disciples of Jesus Christ?" Although the question can be worded several ways, it would be a mistake to think the answer is only a matter of changing individuals. The goal is also to shape congregations into mature manifestations of Christ's body. Thus Paul writes to the church at Ephesus:

> The gifts he gave were that some would be apostles, some prophets, some evangelists, some pastors and teachers, to equip the saints for the work of ministry, for building up the body of Christ, until all of us come to the unity of the faith and of the knowledge of the Son of God, to maturity, to the measure of the full stature of Christ. (Ephesians 4:11-13)

The apostle goes on to say that it is unity in love that "promotes the body's growth" (4:16). Thus, the purpose of this chapter is to: (1) examine the role of pastoral leadership in this process, (2) identify the stages involved as a congregation moves from dream to mission, and (3) explore some ideas for producing a congregation of maturing disciples involved in ministry that glorifies Christ.

Pastoral Leadership for Change

Three leadership priorities can be identified as foundational for pastors of smaller churches who lead their congregations through the transitions into new life as effective centers of Christian ministry. The first is the almost unconscious value they place on momentum. Like coaches of athletic teams, they realize everything cannot be changed all at once, but without a sense of momentum there will be little chance of defeating the demon of discouragement. Their second priority is flexibility, or what has sometimes been called situational leadership. They readily shift from one style or function of leadership to another as required by the situation at hand or how far along the congregation is in its transition to a fully functioning center of ministry. Third, their leadership is shaped by the belief that the ultimate goal is full transformation of persons and the congregation itself into manifestations of God's grace and glory.

1. Leadership as Momentum

Two of my former students, both entering the ministry in midlife, returned from "working the fields" as pastors of smaller churches and came by for a chat. One was packing up his family and leaving a church after his first year. He was discouraged and felt he needed training in "spiritual warfare." He had become snarled in a family feud and felt forced to decide what the church's stand was going to be on a very controversial subject. He bit the bullet, took his stand, served as the prophetic voice of truth, denounced the sin, and was asked to leave. Perhaps the Spirit will use his sacrificial boldness and the church will benefit from this challenge, but there is no way to know.

The other pastor was finishing his third year at his church and glowed as he told of loving and being loved, of reaching people for Christ, and of watching new leadership emerge in a church full of octogenarian gatekeepers. He too was leaving to take a new church but full of excitement that God was doing a new thing and that real change had taken place. Both pastors loved their people, both loved Christ, both wanted to make a difference, both did. But the differences they made are themselves quite different.

When it comes to pastoral leadership that makes the difference called turnaround, is it primarily a matter of the luck of the draw or providence? Not usually, although some churches need much more healing than others. Do successful pastors get good churches to start with? No, rather, they learn to or intuitively know how to walk through minefields and come out on the other side. They choose their battles carefully and don't let others force them into corners. They realize that change comes slowly as Christ, not the pastor, becomes recognized as the head of the body, and as love matures and makes fertile the soil of growth.

Was one of the pastors described above wrong and the other right? No. Did one have it easy and the other have it hard? No. But one may have worked more wisely and made choices with an eye toward the big picture and the long haul. The other chose to resolve a single issue; and although he boldly spoke the truth and drew a line in the sand, he lost the right to keep speaking. He had become the judge and was no longer able to pastor. He told me he now believed "combat" was the proper description of ministry. The other described it as "embracing change with love." One focused on the fight, the other on the future.

These differences are not absolute, but even Jesus knew his ministry was larger than simply being the lamb of God. He had a mission to accomplish with the Twelve and with his other disciples. He spoke boldly, but he also cautioned against judging. He knew when to withdraw as well as when to enter the temple and combat the money changers. Conflict will come, but pastors who create new futures for their congregations seem to understand and practice timing. They function more from a mind-set committed to completing the vision than to announcing final truth and settling disputes. Even Jesus, when once asked to settle a dispute between brothers, replied, "Friend, who set me to be a judge or arbitrator over you?" (Luke 12:14). Turnaround pastors realize momentum is easily sidetracked. Therefore, whenever possible, they stick with their plan and their calling, and avoid pitfalls that lead to divided loyalties and win/lose contests of authority.

2. Leadership as Flexibility

Turnaround pastors in our study described their top six leadership functions as (1) visionary, (2) enabler/encourager, (3) partner/friend, (4) facilitator, (5) cheerleader, and (6) transformational leader. Although the question as worded did not ask for multiple answers, many of these pastors seemed to understand that being successful as a visionary—enabling the vision to become a reality—requires multiple leadership functions. Some approaches are more helpful in the early days of change; others are more appropriate in the stages that follow. Effective leadership committed to momentum adjusts as the conditions dictate.

Several indicated they initially functioned more as visionaries, initiators, and cheerleaders but later shifted to become teachers, administrators, and equippers. One pastor confessed, "I'm mostly a democratic leader, but sometimes I have leaned toward 'benevolent dictator' to initiate change." Another writes: "My roles have changed from being an initiator and solo staff person to becoming an equipper and leader of volunteer staff. Once I had to do most everything; now I am primarily a vision leader and teacher." These pastors seem to understand that appropriate leadership is what is needed at the moment for the sake of momentum. Their leadership is flexible, not a single style or predefined role or function that will remain the same while everything else around it changes.

Flexibility in style of leadership has been studied by a number of researchers in the management and human development field. Paul Hersey and Kenneth Blanchard developed a model they called "Situational Leadership," calling for various blends of relational support and task instruction based on the ability and willingness of the workers. Our use of the word *flexibility* is not identical to the concept of situational leadership as described by Hersey and Blanchard, but it is similar.

It might even be argued that Jesus exercised a form of situational leadership with his disciples. He began his ministry with the twelve disciples by teaching them and showing them what was required in kingdom ministry (Luke 5–8). As their understanding of the task and their intimate relationship with Jesus increased, he sent them out on their own to try their wings at kingdom ministry (Luke 9:1-9). They returned to him and discussed and evaluated all they had experienced (Luke 9:10). Later, seventy are reported to have been sent on a similar mission and returned to reflect with Jesus on the success of the mission and to celebrate the results (Luke 10:1-20). Finally, John reports that Jesus told his disciples it would be better for them if he departed so that the Holy Spirit could come to be their guide and comforter

(John 16:7-13). Although his love for them remained constant, the way Jesus led his band of followers was flexible, depending on their needs and their readiness for responsibility.

Successful shepherds of his flock today seem to follow their master's example. They understand the big picture and accept their place in it as a key to change, but they realize they have different roles to play as momentum is established and the congregation progresses through various stages of revitalization on the way to maturity. The goal is "everyone mature in Christ" (Colossians 1:28). This is the transformational goal, and leaders committed to this goal are transformational leaders.

3. Leadership as Transformation

Many studies have been done on leadership, and hundreds of definitions of the term have appeared in print. But one of the more helpful recent typologies of leadership is that offered by historian and political scientist James MacGregor Burns. Burns was the first to describe the difference between transactional and transformational leadership.[2] Transactional leaders want clear lines of authority and power, and function in terms of an exchange, or a transaction. They want their followers satisfied, but mostly in order to fulfill their own personal goals of success. Their approach is "You give me something and I'll give you something." Robert Cueni suggests in his book *The Vital Church Leader* that a pastor functioning as a transactional leader might offer "God's grace in exchange for a healthy contribution, or encourage people to unite with the church as a way to enhance their social standing and to build the pastor's evangelism record."[3] At best, transactional leaders think in terms of fulfilling a contract, being successful, and doing the job for which they were hired. At worst, they focus only on measurable outcomes, they accumulate power, they seek to promote dependency, and they try to reduce the influence of others so they can control every situation. Transactional leaders can become highly manipulative, impersonal, and even exploitative.

Transformational leadership is based on mutual enhancement, not a one-for-one exchange that is developed out of self-interest. The goal of transformational leaders is to inspire followers to a higher level of participation and satisfaction. They serve as moral agents who facilitate change while encouraging and elevating others to greater levels of responsibility. They are often described as movers and shakers, visionaries, intellectual leaders, leaders of reform, innovators, and even heroes.[4]

This is the type of leadership exercised by turnaround pastors. They are investing in people and in a vision. They adjust to the changing needs of their congregations and their communities. Their pleasure is not in securing a name for themselves but in seeing others grow and become empowered and excited about serving Christ. They try to adjust their own roles and styles of leadership based on the needs of others. They seek to elevate followers into leaders and enable all to function as true Christian disciples. This is their vision for the churches they serve, and this is what they commit themselves to with all the faith, hope, and love they can offer.

Sharon, pastoring in Florida, entered the ministry in midlife. It is easy to see her transformational vision for ministry in these comments: "God has given me gifts that can be used effectively in proclaiming the gospel, and I desire above all else to help others know God's love and transforming power. I long to see the body of Christ grow and thrive."

Phillip, a second-career pastor in Arkansas, revealed a similar commitment to partnership in ministry and being a leader among leaders: "I defined myself as a leader in worship and a partner in ministry. I wrote, taught, and preached positively without being autocratic or dictatorial. I invited response and expected leadership of the laity."

These pastors, many of whom have sacrificed comfort, professional status, and financial security to follow God's call, are in the ministry not because they see it as a way "up" for themselves but because they long with all their hearts to see others succeed and be transformed. They are transformational leaders.

4. Put Them All Together

Although we have been describing three priorities in the leadership styles of pastors acknowledged as successful change agents, the priorities are not entirely separate from one another.

In reality and in practice, they overlap considerably and interact to produce what might be called simply pastoral leadership for revitalized congregations.

James Kouzes and Barry Posner have collaborated to produce a description of the behaviors and commitments of those they label exemplary leaders.[5] Their list of practices closely resembles the activities and values described by the pastors in our study. According to Kouzes and Posner, exemplary leaders:

1. **Challenge the process** by seeking out new opportunities, pioneering, innovating, experimenting, taking risks, and viewing mistakes as learning experiences.
2. **Inspire a shared vision** by looking toward but beyond the horizon; by remaining hopeful, positive, expressive, genuine; by being good communicators; by building on mutual interests toward a common purpose; and by enlisting support from others.
3. **Enable others to act** by nurturing relationships based on mutual trust and respect, by involving others in planning and decisions, by fostering collaboration, and by working to strengthen others.
4. **Model the way** by being clear about their own values and beliefs, by modeling the behavior they expect from others, by planning thoroughly, by clarifying achievable steps, and by creating opportunities for small wins and achievable goals.
5. **Encourage the heart** by recognizing accomplishments and contributions, by expressing appreciation and pride, by celebrating achievements, by nurturing team spirit, thus inspiring continued efforts to work for the vision.

Frequently, these are the very words and images used by turn-around pastors. Not that they are perfect examples or think of themselves as "exemplary leaders," but they work at it, and they count it all a privilege as they help their churches grow into Christian maturity "from one degree of glory to another" (2 Corinthians 3:18).

From Vision to Mission

How do these pastors lead their congregations from the earliest steps of affirmation, encouragement, and dreaming, through whatever it takes to become transformed into exciting centers of ministry and mission? Their answers are not all the same, but three key elements keep recurring: (1) they have their own personal vision and dream for the church, (2) they encourage the dreams of others and facilitate a common vision for the church's future, and (3) they develop a clear and purposeful direction for the church through some form of strategic planning.

1. They Have a Dream

In one of the wonderful old Charlie Brown cartoons by Charles Schulz, Lucy has enticed Charlie Brown into a conversation by reducing her rates for "Psychological Help" from 25 cents to a nickel per hour. Lucy opens the dialogue by comparing life to a cruise ship. The passengers, she says, place their chairs in different places around the ship, depending on their particular outlook on life. Some want to be up front, where they can scan the horizon for good things to come. Some prefer to sit in the back, looking with nostalgia upon where they've been. She concludes by asking her patient where his deck chair is placed. In typical Charlie Brown fashion, he replies that he can't get his deck chair unfolded.

Pastors leading revitalized smaller churches recognize this scenario. Without exception, they would unfold their chairs up front, because that is where hopeful people who want to see where they are going choose to set up their chairs. Actually, they also invest a great deal of time and energy helping others get their chairs unfolded, and then call as many as will follow to move with them to the bow of the ship. Occasionally, they visit with those who prefer the stern, and they celebrate the memories of times and places left behind; but as captains of the ship, they believe the most important view is toward what is coming, not toward what has been.

By no means do all of these pastors start their first conversation with the announcement "Come to the front of the ship!" but some do. In fact, one pastor in downtown Los Angeles wrote a two-page open letter to the officers and members of the church he had been appointed to, informing them of his approach to ministry and his dream for the church even before he arrived for his first Sunday. Included in the letter were the following thoughts:

> *How does your pastor view his members? You are not someone to do my thing on, you are my thing. You will never be an interruption of my work, but are the purpose of my work. My mission is clear as outlined by Jesus when he said to Simon Peter, "If you love me, feed my sheep." There is no room in the Church of Jesus Christ for some members to get special treatment over others. Every name on the roll of the church is a very special person whether he/she is a disgruntled member, a member who has left the church, a member with a grammar school education, or a member with a Ph.D. Therefore:*
> 1. *I am not interested in negative news about others.*
> 2. *I am not interested in how much experience, prestige or power one has unless these things are tied into and in concert with Jesus Christ governing our decisions.*
> 3. *I am not interested in where we are now, or where we were five weeks, five months, or five years ago, but where God can lead us to from here.*
> *It is not enough just to trust God to get things moving. For new things to come to pass we must act on the trust we claim we have. We can soar to new heights by being bold, brazen, and daring in Jesus Christ.*

The pastoral letter continued and established the centrality of the Bible, called for a church-wide conference, announced the start of a new second worship service at 8:00 Sunday mornings, and requested the hanging of a new, colorful, professionally printed banner declaring "The Church Where Jesus is the Star, and the Bible has Center Stage." Then, in closing, the pastor instructed the members that he would be calling on all sick and homebound members immediately, and that he wanted to organize the membership of the church into a caring network of classes.

Although very few pastors would use this jump-start approach to help clarify their own personal vision, almost all of the turnaround pastors described their own dreams and visions for their churches from the earliest days of their arrival. Another pastor wrote:

I walked into that little run-down church where they paid me thirty-five dollars a week and I saw a holy place which God had given me to have a ministry. You have to dream God's dream. See the "beauty" in the "beast" and they will act beautiful. A positive pastor in a negative church can turn it around in three years. A negative pastor in a positive church can destroy it in three months. I never saw a church empty. I always saw it full.

Pastors who make a difference have a dream and see a vision of the way things can be. They don't deny the way things are, but they exude a confidence about the way things are going to be.

2. They Facilitate a Common Vision

When effective pastors lead from their own visions, they are energized for ministry. But for an entire congregation to be energized for ministry requires the dream and the vision to be caught and shared by all—or at least a group of key movers and shakers. So how do these pastors engender a common vision?

First and foremost they talk about, pray about, and preach about the vision they believe in. They remind people that "the best days of the church are always ahead, not behind." And they function from the premise that the only worthy dream or vision for a church needs to be based "on God's ability not human ability." Billy seemed to use this approach. He wrote:

The former pastor left in an angry tirade. I came with humor and joy, talking about dreams and vision. At first there was disbelief. But the people caught the vision and started inviting friends and acquaintances, and we budgeted for growth. We started Sunday school classes without any students so that when they showed up, they would have a class.

Perhaps this is what the writer of Hebrews had in mind when writing: "Now faith is the assurance of things hoped for, the conviction of things not seen" (11:1).

Some of the dreaming and visioning in these churches is mostly a matter of regaining a sense of hope and power, more a matter of a new "image" than a written statement. But many of the pastors actually helped their people create a vision statement. Dennis helped his congregation in Pennsylvania create a "Dream Statement," which envisioned their church as "being the focal point of our community in terms of meeting needs; filled with people and helping young people carry forth the faith."

Sometimes the vision was recorded more like a short motto for the quality of ministry or the type of church the congregation wanted to be known for than it was a formal statement. Two examples were "Making room for our neighbors in the fellowship of faith" and "A warm church that shows the love of God and ministers to all people in a fresh New Testament atmosphere."

Such expressions of a congregation's dream or vision were not necessarily purpose statements or mission statements, but they are related. First a congregation begins to see itself and its future through the eyes of faith and hope, then it can engage in more specific planning and goal setting. The initial congregational vision for a small church in the midst of revitalization is not necessarily the end product of strategic planning. More likely it is only the first fruits. But as some of the sweetness of new life is savored, the congregation is often ready for the additional planning needed for an even greater harvest. These additional levels of development will be examined in chapters 7 and 8, since having a team of leaders who own the vision and the future of the church is critical for maintaining the "beyond" after turnaround.

3. They Develop a Purposeful Direction

The most important step in the success of this process is clarifying the congregational purpose. This is carryover from the dreaming and visioning efforts already mentioned, and is where both the Bible and the prayerful discussions of the members meet. The primary goal is to find the answers to questions like the following: "Who are we?" "Why are we here?" "Whose church is this, anyway?" "What does God expect of us?" "What is our special identity and contribution to this community?" "How can we be faithful to our heritage in a new day?" "Who are the people God desires us to be responsible for in mission?" "How will we witness for Christ?" "What are we expecting God to do among us in the days ahead?"

Some pastors begin by asking such questions informally to key people in their congregations, just to get the ball rolling. Some establish a special committee to work on this task after gathering congregational input and census data or other community information. But almost all believe that finding their identity and God's purpose for them in the Bible is most important. Many denominational planning resources, as well as books on church leadership, offer models for arriving at and writing a purpose statement. Some of these statements are quite elaborate, but most are a few carefully chosen phrases or sentences addressing such areas as worship, witness, outreach, nurture, discipleship, stewardship, and caring for the needs of others.

A strong purpose or mission statement (1) builds morale by reducing the tension of competing claims; (2) reduces frustration because people now know what is most important; (3) builds cooperation among those inside the church and attracts the interest and cooperation of persons and groups outside the church; and (4) assists in regular evaluation of congregational faithfulness and effectiveness.

After helping the congregation clarify its purpose, turnaround pastors employ various methods of setting goals, solving problems, and planning for change. Planning—at least extensive planning—is not one of the natural things a small congregation does. Small churches are like families, and families normally live from day to day unless a problem comes up. There may be a savings account for the "rainy day," but seldom do families sit down together and write out their dreams, their specific and attainable goals, and their annual- and five-year plans. Most small churches prefer to take things as they come. It is not at all unusual to hear the following sympathies expressed: "Planning is for those larger corporations and businesses, not for families; and here at Love Your Neighbor Church, we really are like a family."

Although such thinking may be natural and rooted in a long history, turnaround churches and their pastors are involved in change; change not merely as something happening to them, but change they intend by God's grace to bring about. "Strategic Planning" sounds much more grandiose than some of the actual efforts may warrant, but even the smallest and most informal turnaround churches seem to be thinking intentionally about the future and putting flesh on the bones of their dreams. They were setting goals and making plans for changes to their facilities and for new programs and evangelistic efforts.

Some pastors like Ruth of West Virginia used a fairly simple problem-solving approach. She wrote:

> *My leadership style at first was to present a problem and allow the people to develop a strategy to deal with it. At first they would have no idea where to begin, so I would quickly lay out three or four alternatives. They would discuss them and come up with one. Now, they present different ways to solve the problems.*

Others have gone through more formal strategic planning processes involving annual planning retreats, printed reports, and even outside consultants. One church in Ohio even created an annual "Manual for Ministry." The first page of one of their recent manuals included the following gems:

Ministry Theme:
"Heart and Hands for Christ"

Introduction:
"Goals are dreams which have gotten dressed in work-clothes." This *Manual For Ministry* represents the dreams, ideas, concerns, and needs that God is bringing before us through each other. "Dreams" are God's gifts offering us His invitation to share God's continuing creative acts in the lives of people. We celebrate God's dreams through us as God's people. We affirm that: "Failing to plan is planning to fail."

Definitions:
1. *Mission:* Discovery of needs based upon the biblical principles revealed through the ministry of Jesus Christ (5 Areas).
2. *Objective:* A bridge to action, ideas formed into plans that guide "dreams" toward fulfillment in accordance with the biblical principles from God's Word within and through us.

---

3. *Target:* Where the rubber meets the road, God's Word and will fleshed out through assignments and accountabilities of persons, dates, places, and costs/funding sources.

Jim served a fairly new Christian Reformed congregation in Florida and used his extensive background in business to lead congregational planning. He said his approach was presenting " 'fork in the road' choices to people, and encouraging them to make the right choice." Their Sunday worship bulletin included a purpose statement labeled "Concept of Ministry." In addition, three congregational "Spiritual Goals" were listed to help both the existing members and new people remember and understand where the church was headed.

These pastors seemed to know how and when to shift from the more informal dreaming and visioning so necessary to establish a positive view of the future, to the more formal purpose and mission statements, and finally to specific ministries related to their chosen goals. Not all approached this journey from vision to mission in the same manner, but the very fact that they succeeded in leading their congregations into new ministry efforts and congregational growth indicates these pastors were not just visionaries and dreamers. They knew how to help people see the implications of their prayers and dreams, clarify their God-given purpose, and "put on the workclothes" of goals, planning, and implementation.

Developing a Congregation of Maturing Disciples

Kouzes and Posner, in listing the five behaviors and commitments of exemplary leaders mentioned earlier, indicated such leaders enable others to act, and they model the way. Pastors of turnaround smaller churches have a deep commitment as transformational leaders to developing leadership in others. In addition, they highly value the biblical mandate to "make disciples" and they define success in terms of developing mature disciples as well as reaching out to make new disciples. From the first moment new believers or transferring members are welcomed into the fellowship of these churches, they indicate they feel at home and yet challenged to give of their best and discover the joy of living life at a new level.

What do the pastors of these churches do to help this happen? First, they know how to create a special atmosphere of warmth and welcome in God's grace. Second, they emphasize Christian discipleship and the process involved in growing up into all we are meant to be as mature Christians. Third, they believe in discovering and employing each person's gifts for ministry. Fourth, they understand the need for creative interaction between larger gatherings of the whole congregation and small groups for nurture and growth. Finally, they help their members discover how to live and how to serve God in the larger world.

1. Create an Atmosphere of Welcome

Perhaps it is only natural that pastors who see their second and third most important gifts for ministry—after preaching—as loving people and having people skills should be able to make newcomers and old-timers alike feel wanted and welcomed. But any of us who have been in these situations realize it is not necessarily easy. Long-term members sometimes feel they are losing control with the arrival of new people and they do not always communicate a warm welcome. Even persons who sincerely say, "How good it is to have you with us!" sometimes only speak the words and aren't sure what actions are needed to make the sounds become a song. Welcoming new people is not easy, even for those who love company.

One of the reasons is that church visitors and new members in small churches are not just "company." Rather, they are potential or actual new family members waiting to be adopted. Making company feel welcome is a much different and less demanding task than adopting new family members. New members bring their own set of problems still to be worked out, and most families feel they already have enough of their own.

It might be reassuring to look again at Acts and Paul's letters to notice that all was not smooth and wonderful in the early church. Some particular passages to note are Acts 5:1-11; 6:1-7; 15 (including verses 36-41); Romans 14–15:13; 1 Corinthians 1:10-31; 12; 13; and 14; 2 Corinthians 5:12–6:1; Ephesians 4; and Philippians 2. Why did Jesus pray so intently for our unity (John 17:20-24) and why did Paul write so often about love, oneness in the Spirit, and welcoming one another if it was so easy? In fact, when it did happen, it was its own kind of miracle and convinced many of the priests (Acts 6:7) to join in this new faith. The same sign of God's power seems to be at work today in churches that have leaders who work hard to help create the welcome that is needed.

From the initial contact with new people, multiple efforts are made to help them feel wanted. They find a building that looks clean, cared for, and ready for visitors; sometimes they even find a special "Visitor" parking space right near the door; they see attractive signs giving good and accurate information, and colorful bulletin boards displaying pictures of new members and achievements to celebrate; they see people go out of their way to introduce themselves and they are introduced to everyone as the worship service begins; they experience during worship a warm, engaging friendship between the pastor and the members; they hear good news from the Bible and sincere prayers for people's needs; they observe that members of the congregation help lead worship as well as occupy the pews; they are invited after the service to other events, classes, choirs, and sometimes even to lunch; in the days following they are visited by laypersons, the pastor, or both; they are brought gifts representing "family love" (pies, cookies, fresh bread, flowers); perhaps they receive a phone call or cards, notes, letters, special brochures, and newsletters; and they are remembered by name the next time they visit. Not bad for starters.

As new people continue to attend worship and perhaps other church activities, they are invited into a conversation with the pastor or to a new members class to discuss the meaning of being Christian, baptism, and joining the church. Most of the pastors indicated they had from one to three personal conversations with those interested in joining, or from four to six weeks of classes. When new people do decide to profess their faith and join, they already feel accepted and part of the family. On the occasion of their baptism or their membership in the church, or both, the event is not merely a formal exercise of two minutes' duration, but a celebration. One church pulled out all the stops and sent formal invitations to a special dinner featuring white tablecloths and china where the new members were warmly celebrated and presented personalized leather-bound Bibles with their names inscribed in gold leaf.

When we love as God loves, it isn't hard to use our creative imaginations and be a little lavish as we throw a wedding party and celebrate new births, new life, new family members, and the mystery of union in love between Christ and his Bride. Small churches actually have a much easier time with this than large churches. It is one of the truly wonderful things about being just the right size to welcome everyone up close and personal.

2. Emphasize Discipleship

Hazel from Florida believes it is always appropriate to remind people of our central purpose as Christ's church. She wrote: "It is important to be intentional about one's relationship to Jesus Christ. Always start a meeting with " 'How can we serve Christ's call to make disciples?' " Disciples follow Jesus. What do we need in the way of Bible study, devotional disciplines, loving and supportive community, reorientation of our limited worldviews, resources, and training to be able to follow where he is leading today? These are the issues and the language often used in churches where new members are kept alive not simply to serve a status quo institution but to be part of a movement of the kingdom of God.

Although "discipleship" is not the only way to describe and emphasize this dynamic understanding of Christian living, it does avoid some passive images regarding church membership. Barbara, a pastor in Michigan, decided it was important enough to declare, "I'm going back through my preaching plan and I am going to preach the whole year on discipleship. I want to get over using the word *volunteer* and start using *disciple*."

Robert, also from Michigan, described several changes his congregation made to emphasize this more transformational dynamic of the Christian life:

We changed the name of "Sunday school" to "Christian Life Hour" and we started weekly "Discipleship Prayer Groups." This church had been in existence for 30 years and has had problems for most of those 30 years. There were six people attending when I became pastor thirteen years ago. We now have 234 members with over 200 in worship. My approach has been to break down the old molds and mind-set, to introduce new methods, and to bathe all efforts in prayer. We also assign someone to personally disciple all new members. The members are taught that they are all ministers of God's Word.

The heart of the matter is that we are all ministers. When being a member means being a disciple, and being a disciple means being a minister, a very different ethos is created for a congregation than when members are seen as merely persons who have joined and then are asked to be volunteers.

In a day when the lifestyles and values of the world exert greater influence and with the growing numbers of those who have no real biblical or Christian framework, the church must be very clear that to be "membered" to Christ is to be connected both to his blessings and his sufferings for a world still needing to be reached with his love and gospel. Revitalized smaller churches are helping this old, old story be heard and sung as a new song, in part because they have learned to speak the language and interpret the meaning of Christian discipleship.

3. Employ Gifts for Ministry

Pastors leading small churches to new life and maturity are intentional about wanting to equip Christ's disciples for special ministries that match their gifts. Often this means knowing how to turn over to laypersons certain responsibilities that may have been initially carried by the pastor. Steve, a Kentucky pastor, reported his goal was training people to be pastors, not laypeople. Several men and women in his church completed a lay speakers program and preached whenever he was absent. A pastor in Louisiana, made a similar commitment:

Initially, I had to take charge in some unstable areas such as Youth Leader, Young Adult Sunday school class, Choir, Bible Study. I am no

*longer in charge of the Sunday school class nor the youth. Hopefully I
will soon be able to relinquish control of the choir. This is a delicate
matter. Sometimes people's feelings get hurt because they think they
should be doing these things. But pay special attention to seeking people with gifts and talents who can do things. Get laypeople more
involved in the worship experience. Use them as lay readers, have
them give the children's sermon, work to achieve a combination of
young and old workers in the church. Let people work.*

But emphasizing gifts for ministry is not only a matter of turning over jobs the pastor once did, it includes what was described
above as "a delicate matter"—knowing how to match gifts with
ministries, and how to include new people in positions of service
and leadership. Fred in Pennsylvania told how he included new
members by making some members-at-large on the board and
using as many as possible as worship leaders. But he declares,
"It's not been without a struggle!"

Although some pastors have tried with varying degrees of success to replace entrenched and uncooperative leaders—especially
treasurers and musicians—with newer, more flexible persons,
most try whenever possible to avoid such confrontations and
emphasize instead creating new opportunities for new people. As
the momentum shifts to accomplishing the new vision, new ideas
and possibilities emerge. It is more beneficial to add opportunities for service and celebrate gifts than to merely try to replace
older leaders with new people. Eric wrote:

*I try to enable people and let them have a part in ministry. I try to help
them see what they can do that will help the church and the community. I try to make every job important, even sharpening pencils for the
attendance registration pads. And I'm not coming up with all the
ideas. They're coming from the congregation. That makes this a really
fun place to be because there's always something to celebrate or enjoy.
What I'm enjoying is finding the talents of people. It brings out stewardship of talents God has graced them with. They have made their
own wooden table for the altar, created the stained glass insets for the
doors, started two new children's choirs, put up a Christmas tree and
invited the whole neighborhood to help decorate it, begun to share
space and some worship with a Chinese congregation, and are talking
of ways they can meet some of the needs of the students at the new
elementary school being built next door.*

It is important for all of us to feel needed and that we are contributing meaningfully to our common vision. Sometimes training is needed. Sometimes job descriptions have to be written. Sometimes all that is required is to get out of the way and let a person who knows how "just do it." But relationships are still more important than tasks alone. We need to do all that is possible to help everyone enjoy his or her fair share of contribution, based on God's guidance and the Spirit's gifts for ministry.

Rick believed that even persons on their way to Christ but not yet Christians had gifts to give and could serve. This created a significant problem for the congregation to resolve. One unmarried couple who were living together began to attend the church. Before they had joined or publicly acknowledged their Christian faith, they were allowed to stand at the door as greeters. One couple who had recently transferred into the church quoted Scripture to and demanded of the church leadership that this couple living in sin be removed from any and all positions of ministry. The matter was taken first to the elders and then to a council meeting. Both bodies affirmed this was their congregational philosophy of ministry. Those complaining were told "Jesus loved the outcasts, the sinners, and the tax collectors and let them serve him. He still does, both before and after they know him as Savior and Lord. Non-Christians and nonmembers are restricted from certain roles in church leadership, but *every* person who wants to can do something!"

The unmarried couple, without knowing of this turmoil, announced the next Sunday their decision to accept Christ and get married. They wanted the entire congregation to come to their wedding. There was great rejoicing at God's wondrous grace. In a four-page letter to the congregation, the pastor affirmed his congregation and their understanding of both God's purpose and God's process. Part of the letter read:

> *Though we know there is much sin in the world, somehow we are shocked when we see it in the lives of those in church. We long for a church that is made up of people who have their lives together and are no longer continuing in sin. The truth of the matter is that that has never been the case. The church does not depend on "pretty good people," the church depends on God's grace. All along the way, for the vilest sinner and the most obnoxious Christian sinner, God draws us to*

Himself. And He does it in little ways. He gives us little opportunities to respond and calls us to fuller commitment to Himself. Likewise, you do "evangelism," inviting people to Jesus, in lots of little ways that take people from where they are and move them in a process towards all that God wants them to be. You encourage each "pre-Christian," those on the way to Jesus but not quite there, as well as each Christian to be in ministry. And before people know it, they have been swept up in God's plan for their lives. Yes, they reach a point where they know and show their personal relationship with Christ but it comes at a point along the way.

If more pastors and churches could understand and practice this preconversion dynamic of God's grace, sometimes called prevenient grace, many more persons seeking God's touch on their lives would find it in our churches.

4. Encourage Small Groups

Many of the turnaround churches testified to the importance of small groups in the development of mature disciples. The book of Acts acknowledges the early church knew the importance of meeting in homes as well as joining together for worship in the temple (Acts 2:46). Most of the great redemptive movements throughout church history have discovered that long-lasting transformation requires the kind of community and accountability best experienced in small cells of four to twelve people. Currently, some are even suggesting that the only truly transforming approach to Christian maturity comes through small groups or cells.[6]

Sometimes members in small churches have felt little need for small groups. But the benefit of small groups is not so much to be found in their numbers as in their interactive and intentional agenda for Christian love, growth, service, and accountability. Small groups allow persons with different needs and interests to explore areas of personal growth and ministry without everyone needing to agree to do so at the same time. Small groups are wonderful training labs for learning more about loving and caring for one another than is possible in the context of congregational worship or even in many Sunday school classes or Bible studies.

Barbara discovered that small groups constituted the best seedbed or incubator for new leaders:

> *Small groups are where I can be with people, and get to know them and have a really personal relationship with them. I'm very intuitive and I see people for what they can be and what they can do. I believe in them even long before they believe in themselves. Sometimes I'm wrong, and that's all right. I will lead the group the first time we go through something like The Workbook of Living Prayer, Disciple Bible Study, or Serendipity, always looking for people's strengths, abilities, and gifts for ministry, and especially for potential leaders. The more we get people into these groups the more leaders emerge. The next time that short-term study is presented, I have one of them lead it. Then I have to shift my time priorities to spend more time working with these leaders and less time leading groups myself. It is wonderful to see people grow into the Christian leaders they are meant to be.*

Small groups provide a safe and nurturing arena for the transforming work of the Holy Spirit. Gifts for ministry can be observed and encouraged by pastors and other church leaders.

5. Engage the World through Loving Service

But perhaps most important, here is where the part of the discipling process Jesus referred to as "teaching them to obey everything that I have commanded you" (Matthew 28:20) can best take place. In large groups, or teaching-talking-preaching kinds of groups, the obedience level is usually restricted to "oughts" and "shoulds." In small groups, five or ten persons can decide to do something, and hold one another accountable. Here people actually pray, bear one another's burdens, read the Bible, and report to one another week after week of what they are learning about being obedient to Christ. And although mission and outreach have already been discussed in the last chapter, small groups are often how persons become involved in this critically important aspect of Christian discipleship. Mission teams, visitation teams, and community ministry teams of all types are themselves usually small groups. Out of their study, prayers, and personal sharing, God leads them to act in joyful obedience, and they experience a whole new understanding of following Jesus. They will never again be content to simply say "Lord, Lord," for they have been changed from one degree of glory to another. More than likely they will be heard saying:

> "Lord, when was it that we saw you hungry and gave you food, or thirsty and gave you something to drink? And when was it that we saw you a stranger and welcomed you, or naked and gave you clothing? And when was it that we saw you sick or in prison and visited you?" And the king will answer them, "Truly I tell you, just as you did it to one of the least of these who are members of my family, you did it to me." (Matthew 25:37-40)

Discipleship and Leadership

The pastors who help bring transformation to smaller churches are themselves persons who believe deeply that God is able to change people and congregations from what they were and what they are to what they are yet to become. They are flexible in their leadership style according to the need, and they are committed to the transformation of others' lives, not just the advancement of their own plans and careers. They stimulate a vision of change through their example as well as their preaching and teaching, and they enable their congregations to clarify their true purpose as well as plan specifically what they can do to make their dreams become reality.

They realize as well that changes in congregations depend on changes in individuals. Committed as they are to the great commission of Jesus to make disciples, they help the congregation become more welcoming, more focused on stretching toward Christian maturity, more invested in using the gifts of every member and nonmember, and more involved in small groups for nurture, accountability, and service. And most of the pastors participating in the study believed they were not only developing disciples but also leaders for the future of the church.

But what happens when these pastors, who have done so much to help their congregations progress into new vitality and new levels of kingdom ministry, move on? What does the long-range picture of these turnaround churches look like? Are the maturing disciples that are becoming new leaders in the congregation prepared enough to keep pressing on? Do the new members truly feel they were adopted into the family, or do they remain on the margins and disappear when the "adopting parent" (known as the pastor) moves on? Do these turnarounds maintain their momentum or turnaround again and head backward? These are questions that we explore in the next chapter, and constitute the concern expressed in the title of this book—*Turnaround and Beyond.*

Questions for Discussion

- Leadership for turnaround in our churches involves both pastors and laypeople. What leadership qualities do you believe are most needed right now from your pastor?

- What leadership qualities are most needed from your lay leadership team?

- Assuming the goal of your congregation is to help make disciples of Jesus Christ, how would you explain what it means to be Christ's disciple?

- How does your church currently help make this kind of disciple? If you could suggest adding or changing anything to better accomplish this goal, what would it be? Why?

- What is the relationship between being a mature disciple of Jesus Christ and being a leader in your church? How is such a relationship best maintained?

CHAPTER 7

Turnaround and Pastoral Transitions

Nevertheless I tell you the truth: it is to your advan-
tage that I go away, for if I do not go away, the
Advocate will not come to you; but if I go, I will send
him to you.   *—John 16:7*

What must it have felt like for those early disciples to
hear Jesus tell them it was better for them if he left?
Everything we read about their readiness for his
departure seems to contradict the confidence Jesus possessed. In
fact, the hours and days that followed this announcement were
filled with all kinds of sliding backward in their faith and their
faithfulness as his disciples. Only after they experienced his
resurrection and the day of Pentecost do we see them begin to
regain their courage and readiness to stand against the fightings
within and fears without. Only after the Advocate comes do
they seem to realize the abiding presence of Jesus promised
when he gave them the Great Commission—"I am with you
always" (Matthew 28:20).

Of course, we can't equate today's transitions of pastoral leadership with the experience of those early disciples when Jesus left
them; but there are similarities and some great lessons to be
gained from the New Testament accounts of their efforts to move
on. But let's begin with what happened to the one hundred turnaround churches when the "turnaround pastors" left.

Looking at Leadership Transitions

Ten years after undertaking the original study, I made an effort to contact all of the churches and pastors who participated. Letters, phone calls, and e-mails were sent to over 150 persons. Twenty-eight of the original pastors responded. Six were still pastoring the same churches and two were working alongside a new pastor. Eighteen pastors not in the previous study but currently serving one of the original congregations responded. Altogether we were able to look at thirty-six of the original churches through fifty-two contacts, including some lay members and other observers. The question I wanted to explore was "Are these churches still making progress in the direction of the turnaround as originally described?" Actually, a few were booming and were no longer small churches. Four had grown significantly and were now averaging 200, 350, 700, and even 1, 700 in worship. One was involved in planting sixty-five churches in six countries, and another had taken over management of the community centers in their city and was offering three worship services with a staff of over thirty full-time and part-time employees. In these churches it was clear that members were excited to become both disciples and missionaries.

Sadly, however, three-quarters of the congregations contacted lost ground and entered a season of decline and conflict. Several had actually closed their doors or were on the brink of doing so. Survival was once again a dominant theme being considered by many, and a few that had suffered losses after one or more pastoral transitions were finally beginning to gain ground again.

The original study made it clear that small, traditional, long-established congregations struggling for survival could be revitalized and experience new life through an exciting season of turnaround. But checking back with these pastors and churches led to new questions. What caused some to maintain the momentum and others to fall back again into decline or even despair? Was it as simple as having or not having the right pastoral leadership? Were the common characteristics and strategies leading to turnaround that were discerned in the original study still valid, or were we much too optimistic? These questions and others deserved answers, and the fifty-two pastoral leaders who returned surveys or were interviewed helped provide valuable new insights for how to maintain the momentum of turnaround. The heart of the matter seems to be "How does any organization best maintain its momentum when a transformation leader moves on?" This is obviously not just a question for churches. We would have to be totally isolated from the world we live in day-in and day-out not to recognize the significance of this question for all kinds of human endeavors. Therefore, before we look more closely at the leadership transitions that constitute the *beyond* for turnaround churches, let's examine what those who have studied this phenomenon in other arenas have to say.

In the Public Arena

Probably no other organization in the United States is more on the front line of addressing the needs of the business world than the Harvard University School of Business. Frequent articles in the *Harvard Business Review* and the newer Harvard Business Online offerings demonstrate a growing interest in this challenging arena of leadership transitions. A quick glance at Harvard Business Online (a shopping center for leadership resources) gives the viewer lots of options to purchase books, courses, and audiovisual resources addressing this topic. One advertisement for the 2004 release of a $149 package under the heading "Proven Strategies for Leadership Transition" by Michael Watkins reads:

> One quarter of managers transition to a new role or job each year. In a large organization, it takes a new leader an average of 6.4 months to become a positive contributor in the new role. Too few managers—and organizations—approach these transitions with a strategic plan. According to leadership expert Michael Watkins, a new leader's success or failure is determined within 90 days on the job.[1]

It's not hard to see why the business world is interested in helping such managers and leaders learn to make their best contribution early—within the first 90 days. There are lots of wonderful articles, conversations, interviews, checklists, strategies, and suggestions in such resources, but it doesn't take long to discern that the for-profit world of business is not much like a small church.

In addition, most of the resources seem aimed at helping the transition leader, not the organization itself, succeed.

Perhaps closer to what we experience in the church is material on leadership transitions published for nonprofit and volunteer-based organizations. One of the key publications in this arena is *The Nonprofit Quarterly*. In a special issue focused on this particular subject, authors Denice Rothman Hinden and Paige Hull comment:

> Leadership transition is gaining the attention of many concerned about the capacity and effectiveness of nonprofits because quality of leadership is widely recognized as a significant variable. . . .
>
> Today, of an estimated 1.6 million nonprofits in the U.S., roughly 10–12 percent are managing a transition in executive leadership at any given time; in some communities this means a hundred organizations annually. . . . Further, according to recent surveys, 15–35 percent of nonprofit executives plan to leave their current positions within two years and 61–78 percent are planning to leave within five years.[2]

Again, it's easy to see that pastoral transitions in our churches seem to be part of the whole leadership scene today. These same two authors go on to say: "The data suggests—and some experience confirms—that transitions occur more frequently and may be more difficult in smaller organizations than in larger organizations with more resources."[3] This observation gets us closer to what many smaller churches have experienced again and again. In fact, often the lead time given to the congregation (both in call and in appointment systems) to secure a pastor comes with very little time for preparation. In order not to disrupt the flow of good things happening, pastors frequently believe it is best not to reveal too much too soon if a move is in the works. But of course, last-minute announcements create their own special problems for everyone.

There is no question that leadership transitions are fraught with risk. The *Executive Transitions Monograph Series* reports:

> During the last decade, field research by the Neighborhood Reinvestment Corporation has highlighted the serious risks of failed or unsuccessful transitions. This work has found that most transitions (as many as 70%) are "non-routine" and occur

due to an organizational crisis or the departure of a founder or visionary leader. This research has also demonstrated that poorly managed executive transitions incur high costs to organizations and communities. Too frequently, there is a repeat executive turnover and extended periods of under-performance. In extreme circumstances, organizations go out of business, leaving a wake of broken commitments and financial entanglements.[4]

The special challenges and frequent failures of transitions involving an organizational crisis or departure of a visionary leader almost make predictable the stories reported at our original turnaround churches during their pastoral leadership changes. Yet there is hope.

One of the key factors contributing to a successful transition in almost all leadership situations studied in the nonprofit sector is the ability of the board or other leadership team to clearly articulate the position opening as a challenge and ask potential candidates to analyze the situation and present their best proposal for how they would creatively address the opportunity. Often the ability to articulate such details is missing in our smaller churches either because the team has not thought in those terms or because they fear there won't be many options anyway. In a call system versus an episcopal appointment, there may be a little more time, energy, and resources for such preparation, but even when call committees begin their work, they often focus much more on getting a preacher than on replacing a leader.

One final contribution on the subject comes from Don Tebbe, senior associate with TransitionGuides, from an article appearing in *TransitionLeader* newsletter.[5] A few of his recommendations include:

1. *Clarify the transition plan and enlist support*—The primary concern here is to establish the priority issues to be examined, clarify the roles various persons will play, and establish the timeline you have to work with.
2. *Prepare the board*—This translates into training those responsible for direct involvement in the search or decision making to know their responsibilities and options.

3. *Prepare the staff*—Thinking in terms of smaller churches, this would mean communicating to the larger body of leaders (and even the congregation) the steps and timeline involved in both the departure of the current pastor and the arrival of the next one.

4. *Prepare the physical environment and systems*—This might mean paying attention to facility adjustments or upgrades that have been put off and addressing any gaps in communication channels or equipment that might be needed because of the change in personnel. Often this is challenging because we aren't even fully aware of how we "do things around here" or what equipment actually may belong to the current pastor.

5. *Plan the handoff and orientation of the new executive*—This includes everything from personal and community announcements and celebrations of the departing executive, to specific assignments for orienting and introducing the new one.

Such skeletal outlines are not by any means a detailed blueprint either for business or nonprofit organizations or for local churches. But research into the success that comes from following similar plans has been going on since the early 1990s, and the results are very encouraging. Several ETM (Executive Transition Management) organizations began to offer consulting services to nonprofits following the principles described above. The results were a significant increase in executive tenure (4.3 to 5.7 years), increased organizational health (from 67% to 89% on a health scale), and enthusiastic support for the process.[6] Transitions in leadership don't have to be as confusing and dangerous to an organization's health as they often have been. This is indeed good news for all of us.

In the Church

In light of the above, it may not be surprising that 75 percent of the turnaround churches experienced struggles and decline during their pastoral leadership transitions.[7] Many of us have experienced this ourselves either as pastors or as members of a congregation. I recall the advice given as I moved from a staff position in a large church to being the only pastor of a smaller congregation that was in a crisis. An older colleague and mentor told me it was fairly simple; I just needed to "visit, visit, and visit for the first six months." I did my best, but soon discovered there were far more dynamics at work than could be addressed by simply making pastoral visits. I was caught in a whitewater whirlpool of confusion, bitterness, and distrust, and no one had bothered to inform me, give me a map to navigate the river, or prepare me for what appeared to be certain death if I didn't bail out. On another occasion, a woman beginning to become very active in our church told me she didn't intend to join because she knew I wouldn't be staying long enough to make it worthwhile. Pastoral transitions can be tough on everyone.

One of the key reasons that pastoral transitions create so much difficulty and potential loss of newer participants in smaller churches is they were not adequately adopted by the family but only by the parent figure represented by the outgoing evangelistic pastor. This showed up again and again in the follow-up research of the original churches. Small churches are indeed like families, and if the growth of newer members in the family is to be maintained, the whole family has to get in on welcoming and making room. This was clearly seen in the church in the New Testament as the Hebrews and Hellenists struggled to connect as one family instead of separate cultural and social parties (see again "Create an Atmosphere of Welcome" in chapter 6). It required the leaders to intentionally make room for those with the least amount of family history. A successful pastoral transition involves more than just caring for the outgoing and incoming pastors. This is why turnaround churches with a greater emphasis on making disciples rather than on getting more members make it through these transitions easier.

It is fitting that "transitions" has become a common theme in literature produced for the church as well as for the profit and non-profit sectors. Much of this literature is aimed at helping a new pastor successfully navigate the swirling waters and certainly would have been helpful to me those many years ago. This material can be a lifesaver for an incoming pastor and is often quite helpful to the congregation as well, but materials prepared primarily for the congregation and its leaders seem to be more sparse. And when we consider the total picture of pastoral transitions, there are actually three parties involved: the pastor leaving, the congregation, and the pastor coming. We can now say with certainty that all three circles of influence are critically important if turnaround churches are to make it across the great divide and continue to thrive with a momentum that honors and glorifies Christ.

1. The Outgoing Pastor

The intent here is not to address all possible situations that lead to pastoral transitions but to focus on congregations that have experienced turnaround with the help of a gifted and respected visionary-pastor who has decided to move on. This means that the outgoing pastor has done many things right and more than likely secured the goodwill of most of the congregation. In fact, often the newer members and those attending but not yet members find it hard to even think of the church without the current pastor. There is bound to be some pain and a sense of loss in the pastoral transition, no matter how successful it turns out to be.

The first thing an outgoing pastor can do is to begin preparing for this event in the life of the church very early on—in fact as early as possible. Most smaller congregations have done very little planning for these eventualities, no matter how often they have been through them. The pastor who is leaving would have done well to help them think through how to manage transitions long before he or she made the announcement of departure. The resistance to thinking this way is twofold. First, the current pastor when arriving was probably totally focused on what her or his own transition consisted of, not the next one. Second, the mere mention of such things might sound like a lack of commitment to the moment at hand and the tenuous new relationship just beginning. If any thought or expression was given to the larger transition process, it was probably something like "We all hope we don't have to go through this again anytime soon."

Longevity of pastoral leadership is unquestionably significant for producing turnaround. Early preparation for the next pastor, however, does not necessarily mean discussing it as if it would soon be occurring again. Rather, it indicates that the pastor knows enough about successful transitions to affirm the helpful ingredients already in place and begin giving attention to those that are missing. More will be said about this as we consider in more detail the congregation's contribution to a pastoral transition. Suffice it to say, there will, in all probability, be another pastoral transition and probably at a time that will surprise almost everyone. Keeping this in mind from the earliest days of a new pastorate will contribute to a healthy and holistic approach to leadership development as well as to managing the enduring success of any turnaround.

It would be helpful for every pastor to recall how both John the Baptist and Jesus approached this task. John declared openly, "He must increase, but I must decrease" (John 3:30) and early on opened the door to the kingdom's leadership being much larger than his own contribution. And Jesus not only trained his disciples to *do* certain things but also to *be* his replacement team ready to step up and lead when the time came. Thus, they gradually learned to trust Jesus, the Holy Spirit, one another, and their gospel. What we see happening in the book of Acts is a special kind of fruitfulness empowered by their mutual experience of gradually being formed into a confident band of leaders in the kingdom of God. Pastoral leaders should ask themselves how well they are doing at creating this sort of leadership core for the future of the congregation.

A second part of the process for the existing pastor is to clarify and review the basic ingredients involved in successful leadership transitions. This can easily be illustrated through changes in leadership positions in the life of the congregation or other churches in the area, but it also allows the pastor to teach critical principles that will be drawn on when the time comes for a pastoral transition. It would be good for this to become an annual review with the key players in the congregation's leadership. In my denomination, The United Methodist Church, clergy are under appointment a year at a time, and part of that process requires annual reviews.[8] Even in a call system, sometime early in the second or third year might be an ideal time to actually start walking through the evaluations that lead to healthy transitions and see it as part of good leadership development.

A third contribution is to let the leadership team know as graciously and as early as possible that the time may be at hand for the next pastor to be secured. Often it is thought best to hold off until the decision is finally made. But none of us like to be totally unprepared for such announcements. In a call system, this gives time to set up the necessary structures for a healthy transition. In an appointment system, it would reduce the unhealthy consequences caused by too many pastors who seem to lay the blame for such moves on the bishop or the superintendent. This is not helpful, nor is it usually even honest. Pastors do have choices, both in a call system and when under appointment. Those under appointment are asked early in the year whether they "prefer to stay," are "willing to move," or "prefer to move." Unless there is an unexpected crisis of some kind, these preferences are usually honored. For a pastor to say she or he is "willing to move" and then say "the bishop is moving me" with no further explanation is being fraudulent, which leads to an adversarial distancing from the benefits of the denominational resources.

A fourth offering the outgoing pastor can make is to be available for a pastor-to-pastor debriefing shortly after the new leader has been selected or arrives. This can be very important, whether the incoming pastor is an interim or full replacement. There are at least a couple of different formats this conversation could take. Nearly twenty years ago, one of my students serving a part-time student appointment shared with me the notebook he prepared for the pastor replacing him. I was impressed with the excellent congregational analysis and pastoral information he included and I asked him where he got the idea. He said, "I thought every pastor would probably do this." I assured him that I wished he were correct, but unfortunately my experience led me to believe it was quite rare. I kept a copy of the notebook and shared it with classes I taught.

Sometimes it is difficult, either because of timing or distances (I replaced a pastor who had been gone for three months and had relocated to another state), for the outgoing and incoming pastors to have detailed, face-to-face conversations about the ministry culture and context of the congregation under consideration. Perhaps cell phones, videoconferencing on computers, and e-mail offer new alternatives to notebooks and face-to-face talks, but the topics of conversation might well include something like the following categories:

Pastoral: A list of members who are angry, hurting, ill, homebound, trusted allies, early adopters, most influential, positive and negative power people, pushing their own agendas, on their way in and up, on their way out or recently departed, and a short history of pastoral leaders and their impact on the church. It might also be helpful to clarify matters related to pastoral housing, family life, days off, vacations, salary, and so on.

Worship: Traditions, rituals, controversies, preaching style, themes focused on over the last year, special occasions, significant spiritual turning points, musical preferences and possibilities, roles of laypersons and various ages in worship, seasonal adjustments, spoken or unspoken dress codes, and attendance trends.

Program: A basic list of offerings for education and growth in discipleship, seasonal events, key leaders already in place and those emerging, opportunities tried but unsuccessful, opportunities ready to be tried, stewardship emphases, outreach efforts, advertising approaches, small groups in place, and programs on hold waiting for pastoral perspective.

Administration: Organizational structure, any recent changes, adjustments considered, committees, report formats, decision-making processes both formal and informal, use of ministry teams, financial trends, facility use and policy, keys, security, and relationships with other congregations or denominational structures.

Leadership/Staff: Secretarial help, paid support staff, unpaid staff positions, job descriptions, approaches to selection and training, inner circle of visionaries, detail persons, areas needing more help, evaluation structure, and confidentiality issues.

Church Culture: Spiritual temperature, overall health, possible land mines, morale, commitment to prayer, understanding of how the Spirit leads, openness to new people and ideas, clarity of vision and mission, existing conflicts, approach to conflict management, comfort with denominational connections, theological identity, comfort with ethnic or cultural diversity, ability to laugh, enjoyment of one another, and awareness of the presence of God at work in their midst.

Mission: Biggest issues, unique ministries, changes in community, primary channels for reaching new people, awareness of place in larger world, investment in world mission, and readiness to go rather than sit.

Other: Add your own.[9]

Many of these matters can be and should be openly discussed in the larger arena of congregational leadership, but the unique perspectives of the outgoing pastor will be exceptionally helpful to the new arrival—even if some will need to be checked out with others in ongoing conversations. Judicatory leaders can likewise be excellent contributors to this discussion.

2. The Congregation

Ultimately what we are working with in the transition process is the ongoing health of the congregation. Therefore, the congregation itself commands the greatest influence over the success of the pastoral transition. Everything indicates that the outgoing pastor in a turnaround church has made a significant contribution. Leadership is critical. But leadership is a mutual responsibility shared both by the pastor and the church. Healthy transitions require healthy activities on the part of all participants, and for the congregation those activities begin with attitude and spiritual disciplines. Carolyn Weese and J. Russell Crabtree write:

> Imagine a church:
> - That is so invested in its mission that it is willing not only to break the taboos and talk about leadership changes but also to manage them
> - With a vision for excellence in managing leadership transitions
> - Where the leadership changes do not blindside or sidetrack the vision
> - Where the vision manages change, rather than change managing the vision.[10]

To this they add: "It is important to state emphatically that the personal and corporate spiritual work required in a successful pastoral transition is critical . . . (and) needs to include the spiritual components of prayer, Scripture reading, personal reflection, confession, and nurture of faith. . . . Transformation is not a function of information, but of exploration with trust."[11] Turnaround churches continue to successfully move forward during leadership transitions by using the same basic tools they employed on the whole journey. The first congregational responsibility is the proper mixture of faith, hope, and love.

Second, the board or staff-parish leaders in the congregation need to have their strategic plan in place and begin to work the plan. Good planning for pastoral transitions begins with good information and a cohesive team of leaders ready to protect and expand their mission for God's glory. If the outgoing pastor has helped prepare for this day, the congregation already has a firm grasp on its vision/purpose/mission statements. The congregation has recently reflected on the changes in the community affecting its mission, it has assessed its own strengths and weaknesses, and it recognizes some of the critical next steps needed for maintaining its momentum. If these factors have not been examined recently, it's time to begin. Almost every judicatory office now has assessment instruments available to check for vital signs and also personnel who can assist in this process.[12]

Third, proceed with implementation of the rest of the pastoral transition plan. The steps involved will no doubt have appropriate denominational variations, but the major themes are as follows:

1. Remember that prayer and dependence on the Holy Spirit is at the heart of the entire process.
2. Make sure the appropriate committee is in place and informed of procedure.
3. Establish a tentative time line and a checklist of assignments.
4. Meet with appropriate judicatory staff, or consultants, or both.
5. Determine if the replacement should be made as soon as possible, or if extra time to process the transition decision could be helpful. In a call system, and now more frequently in the appointment system,[13] this will include reflection on whether or not to pursue an interim pastor.

6. Communicate, communicate, and communicate again with all parties involved, including the congregation.
7. Prepare the celebration honoring the contributions of your outgoing pastor.
8. Engage in the selection or consultative process, making use of all of the report materials prepared in step 2.
9. Prepare the celebration welcoming your new pastor.
10. Listen, pray, share one another's dreams and visions, offer helpful feedback, and keep focused on being the body of Christ for the sake of the world.

This process is one that some congregational leaders will feel comfortable with or at least will find familiar. Other leaders or committee members may be newer participants in the life of the church and find it quite challenging. Whatever the case, the heart of process is bringing to the table good information, committing to bring one's best to the task, and maintaining agreed-upon confidentiality, as well as having confidence that this can be a deeply rewarding experience for the entire congregation and its mission in the world.

3. The Incoming Pastor

The first thing the incoming pastor should do is express gratitude to God and the congregation for the opportunity to serve humbly in the name and for the glory of Christ in this new context. Very helpful in establishing mutual confidence in the decisions that have been made is sharing how God has been at work in the pastor's life. This involves telling his or her faith story, including earliest memories of wanting to serve God, persons influential in discovering the meaning of amazing grace, experiences that led to a call to pastoral ministry, understanding of the nature and purpose of the church, special gifts and graces that will be helpful at this stage in the life of the congregation, and, when appropriate, a full introduction to the pastor's family. This kind of sharing is both a natural and expected personal witness and an opportunity for informal conversation, questions and answers, lightness, laughter, and a joyful celebration of God's providence and the Spirit's leading in our lives.

As a second part of this expression of gratitude, the pastor should affirm the work of his or her predecessor(s) and the steps of faith boldly taken by the congregation. Jesus himself is our model for this. In appropriate moments he strongly affirmed John the Baptist with words like "I tell you, among those born of women no one is greater than John" (Luke 7:28a). Unless a pastor is beginning a brand-new congregation (and even then), others have led the way and opened doors for the kingdom. This is especially true in the churches we have described as turnaround churches. As the body of Christ we are together on a journey, pressing on toward the prize, and we will do well to affirm what Paul counseled the church at Corinth:

> I planted, Apollos watered, but God gave the growth. So neither the one who plants nor the one who waters is anything, but only God who gives the growth. The one who plants and the one who waters have a common purpose, and each will receive wages according to the labor of each. For we are God's servants, working together; you are God's field, God's building.
>
> (1 Corinthians 3:6-9)

A third important step for a new pastor is revealed in what follows immediately after Jesus' affirmation of John cited above. The whole verse in Luke 7:28 reads: "I tell you, among those born of women no one is greater than John; yet the least in the kingdom of God is greater than he." There is always more to come; and in the kingdom, we celebrate both the old and the new, the past and the future, the already and the not yet. In the words of Jesus, "the kingdom of heaven is like the master of a household who brings out of his treasure what is new and what is old" (Matthew 13:52). Affirming what has gone before is preparation for what Christ still has in store. Perhaps at this point in a new ministry it is still too early to predict what this might be, but this is an opportune time for the new pastor to affirm the hopes and dreams revealed in the materials prepared by the congregational transition team, as well as to cast a bit of his or her own vision. It's the continuity between what God has already done and faith in what lies ahead that makes the transition a new birthing to be received and celebrated.

Fourth, the new pastor needs to invest in careful listening. This involves both listening to the current leaders and others in the congregation, and to whatever might prove helpful or need to be clarified by the previous pastor. This may well be a structured listening held with various small groups of persons invited to the pastor's home or hosted in a member's home, or it may be more like an informal effort to contact individuals and families one by one. There are some real benefits, however, in using the small-group approach. One pastor in Florida suggested the following model:

1. *Invite groups of eight to ten to the parsonage.*
2. *Give out name tags, ask them to fill out their full name and any nickname.*
3. *Ask the participants to introduce themselves by name* (they can also provide a story of how they got their name and any special nicknames). Or ask a "preference question," such as:
   - *favorite ice cream or favorite vacation in their whole life*
   - *most meaningful Christian experience* (a time of laughter and tears, and a reminder of God's ability to meet us in special ways).
4. *Ask them to imagine the following "time machine" situation:*
   - *Hand out a special card with room to answer the question posed.*
   - *Explain that each of them is "taken away" in the time machine for five years.*
   - *Ask them, "On your return, as you step out, what do you see happening if God's vision for our church is taking place?"*
5. *Hold a retreat with leaders.*
   - *Share the ideas collected and discuss how well they align with the existing values, vision, and mission of the congregation.*
   - *Prayerfully discern any new steps to take as the leadership team in responding to the vision images collected and their possible impact on the future of the congregation.*

Listening is not an abandonment of leadership responsibilities but rather a way to discern with greater confidence the leading of the Spirit, as well as a way to build trust and enhance mutual investment in a shared future. As a new pastor, all of these benefits are invaluable in establishing a renewed culture of faith, hope, and love.

Looking to Beyond

Pastoral transitions are frequently dangerous to the health and well-being of congregations. They are among the giants that can (and should) strike some fear in the hearts of God's people. They need to be approached with great care and prayer, and like the young David, with a sense of trusting in the God who has delivered us in the past and will do so again. Each player in the process has an important contribution to make, but this is never merely a matter of activities on a checklist. More than anything else, smaller congregations that are going to survive and thrive in the future need to develop a wonderfully cohesive leadership team that has come to the point where they love, learn, and lead together. They think of themselves first and foremost as disciples of Jesus and partners with the Holy Spirit.

If the church in any form (and especially in the form of smaller congregational gatherings) is to joyfully glorify God as it carries out its God-given mission in today's world, it must find a way to build a radically committed core of leaders who are responsible for the well-being of the faithful as well as for informed and compassionate outreach to their communities. How to assist in the formation of these teams is what we explore next, including a look at one new movement called into being in order to help smaller congregations all across America (and beyond) become churches that are

> *Abiding in Christ,*
> *Advancing God's Mission*
> *Alive in God's Glory.*[14]

Questions for Discussion

- Identify a time in your life when it was difficult to say goodbye to someone. What part does that person play in your life today?

- Pastoral transitions can be especially difficult times for smaller congregations. Why would you say this is the case?

- What was your best experience of a pastoral transition? What made it work?

- How ready are you for the next one? What steps could your leadership team be taking now to ensure the best success?

- Since longer tenure of turnaround leaders has long been recognized as contributing to sustaining both momentum and growth, how could you encourage this?

CHAPTER 8

Turnaround and Beyond—Abiding

I am the vine, you are the branches. Those who abide in me and I in them bear much fruit, because apart from me you can do nothing. —John 15:5

During my first year in seminary, the chaplain of the United States Senate, the Reverend Dr. Richard Halverson, spoke in chapel. Frankly, I don't remember his message, but I do remember what we talked about when I scheduled a personal conversation with him later in the day.

Because of my fairly recent experience with Christ, nothing seemed more important to me than personal evangelism and the amazing wonder of helping another person come to trust him as living Lord and Savior. As we talked, he challenged that perspective. His comment to me was, "I like your zeal, but there is only *one* ultimate responsibility for the Christian, and it is not what you think. The only thing you *must* do as a Christian is abide in Jesus."

I argued for a while, confident that he had to be either too liberal or too spiritual for my taste. Finally, I decided that even though he was wrong, I would have to leave it at that since I couldn't seem to change his mind. In parting, he pointed me to chapter 15 in John's Gospel and suggested that I read the first seventeen verses carefully. Eventually, I did. I was converted! This passage has become my treasure.

A Little Biblical Background

When Jesus drew on this image of being the "true vine," he was connecting his disciples with one of the great Old Testament symbols for the nation of Israel, an image he found useful for several of his parables about the kingdom. Israel was the "vine" God had taken out of Egypt (Psalm 80) and planted in a choice and promised land. As the Gardener, God had watered, pruned, and protected his vine to ensure its abundant harvest, but always the fruit amounted only to puny, pea-sized, worthless clusters of bitter grapes gone wild (Isaiah 5:4 and Jeremiah 2:21). God's chosen people, Israel, were obviously not God's true vine.

So Jesus declares to his disciples, "I am the True Vine . . . and you are my branches . . . but unless you abide in me—remain intimately connected to me—you can do nothing; however, if you abide in me and my cleansing word abides in you, and if you let the divine Gardner—my Father—prune you, you will be wonderfully fruitful for the glory of God as my disciples; and you will delight my Father and yours, and joyfully know our love flowing in you" (John 15:1-11, author's translation).

There is more in these verses than space allows us to fully examine, but here is a quick introduction. When the North African theologian Tertullian first gave us the word *trinity* to describe the union and diversity of the Father-Son-Spirit nature of God, he likened the Holy Trinity to "the root, the shoot and the fruit." To carry this further: the Father, that none has seen, is like the invisible Root out of which all life springs. The Son, that grew up in our midst as the "Shoot" out of the stump of Jesse (Isaiah 11:1-9), is the True Vine, and reveals the Father, as well as sending forth from himself many branches to bear the fruit of God. The Spirit, who is the Love of God in Person, flows from the Father and the Son like a Holy Sap out of the Root, through the Vine, into branches that abide, and produces fruit—the fruit of the Holy Trinity, the fruit of the Spirit, the fruit of the gospel inviting ever more branches to become engrafted, cleansed, pruned, and fruitful.

All disciples of Jesus are thus branches designed and equipped to bear much fruit and glorify the Father in heaven (John 15:8). How does that happen? The process—using the metaphor of God's vine—includes:

Cleaning (v. 3): This is what a vinedresser does in preparation for the growing season and it means radically cutting back the branches for a whole new beginning, a new season of life and growth. This is what Jesus says he accomplishes through his Word.

Abiding (vv. 4, 6, 7, 9, 10): Keeping the flow of the Holy Spirit open by walking in the presence of the Lord and living in full awareness that the mystery is this: "Christ *in* you, the hope of glory" (Colossians 1:27, emphasis added). This is how we bear Christ's fruit, for unless his life and love is flowing in us, we can do nothing.

Pruning (v. 2): The vine grower-gardener knows that apart from pruning, branches produce less fruit and more leaves, and the vine goes wild. Pruning means cutting off the extraneous, the life-absorbing periphery that settles for a little fruit while ignoring the reality that God is glorified by much fruit.

Loving (vv. 9-10): Love is the nature of God, the nature of the flow, the nature of the gospel, the nature of the fruit, and the nature of our obedience. Apart from this love, we are nothing and can do nothing. We are only raisins drying in the sun.

Joyful living (v. 11): The outcome of this kind of living is much fruit that glorifies God, but also joy for each disciple. These commands are not given to make our lives difficult, but rather so that the same joy that Jesus knows will completely fill us and spill out for others. The joy of the Lord is our strength, *and* our reward.

A Short Story

One Sunday when I was preaching on this text, I wanted to help make this concept real for the children too. As they came forward to sit on the steps for the children's time, I picked up a very large and lusciously ripe pear and began to munch and slurp in front of the children. No one said a word as they sat down. I continued to noisily enjoy my pear until one child finally broke the silence and boldly declared, "You aren't supposed to do that." "What?" I asked. "Eat in front of people unless you are going to share," he replied. I asked if he would like a bite. He said he would, so I offered him my pear. I asked if any others liked pears and wanted a bite. Lots of hands went up, so I began to move down the row of children rotating the disappearing pear each time another child took a nibble.

As I neared the end of the line, another small boy whose hand had been quite high, looked at what was left of the pear and jerked his hand behind his back. I asked if wanted a bite. He replied, "I did, but I don't." I inquired why he had changed his mind. He assured me he had been taught "not to eat where everyone else had already been." With a smile (and of course the whole congregation listening intently), I asked if he liked pears. He energetically told me he did, so I asked if he would like a bite of pear if I gave him one of his very own. "*Sure,*" he almost shouted. Reaching in my big pocket I produced another pear and passed it to him. With a great delight dancing in his eyes, he placed the pear to his lips, tried to bite it, and then . . . gave it back to me. "It's plastic," he groaned. I exclaimed, "Oh, no! Is it really?" He earnestly assured me that it was, so I took it from him and under careful examination I had to agree, it was plastic.

I told him that I would get a real one for him right away (which I did), but first I wanted to ask him something. "Why did you try to eat a plastic pear?" His answer was stunningly penetrating, "Because you gave it to me, and it looked real."

I chatted a few more minutes with the children about what had just happened and shared what Jesus told his disciples in John 15 about *real* fruit. But the priceless insight from that one child gave all of us a sermon beyond my wildest hopes. How often we in the church become tempted and even quite good at producing "artificial fruit." It looks real, and we give it out to people, but it's not full of the fresh juice of life that tastes like Jesus. In fact, it's just "religious" or "good hearted" or "churchy." As such it can never satisfy people's deepest longings and hungers to "taste and see that the LORD is good" (Ps. 34:8). This kind of fruit can only come from a living, abiding connection with the true source, Jesus—the only channel of divine love. Thus, unless we abide in him, he assures us, "you can do nothing" (John 15:5), nothing that really matters. What really matters is love, the love of God flowing into us as his branches and producing much fruit to feed a hungry world.

John Wesley used a different image for this love, but as he traveled about and saw the crowds with the eyes of Jesus (Matthew 9:35-38), he wrote:

We see—and who does not?—the numberless follies and miseries of our fellow creatures. We see on every side either men of no religion at all or men of a lifeless, formal religion. We are grieved at the sight, and should greatly rejoice if by any means we might convince some that there is a better religion to be attained, a religion worthy of God that gave it. And this we conceive to be no other than love: the love of God and of all mankind; the loving God with all our heart and soul and strength, as having first loved *us*, as the fountain of all the good we have received, and of all we ever hope to enjoy; and the loving every soul which God hath made, every man on earth, as our own soul.

This love we believe to be the medicine of life, the never-failing remedy, for all the evils of a disordered world, for all the miseries and vices of men.[1]

The fruit of this divine love flowing through us is salvation, transformation, and the medicine of life. Whatever else we are about in our churches, unless we are abiding in this love and offering it to each other and to all, we are doing nothing. The turnaround we have been examining throughout this book is ultimately about nothing else. But when the flow of this Holy Sap from the Root through the True Vine is blocked or misdirected or forgotten, we have a tendency, at best, to produce more leaves and less fruit. What can help ensure that none of the obstacles we looked at earlier, and not even leadership transitions, will turn us backward again? How can we have turnaround and beyond—turnaround that lasts?

A Quest for Answers

In December 2004 a two-day consultation was held at Asbury Theological Seminary on the future of the small-membership church. Sixteen persons from five denominations attended. The goal of the occasion was not to propose a program or a solution to the challenges facing hundreds of thousands of churches, but to prayerfully ask the question, "What might God be saying to some of us who value these congregations, regarding their possible role in the kingdom over the next few decades?"

A proposal emerging from the event was that perhaps some of us, those interested and able, ought to commit ourselves to meeting together once a month to prayerfully explore how we might design a renewal model and a revitalizing movement among thousands of smaller churches across the United States. Twelve indicated an interest, eight persons made the commitment to invest the long-term time and energy, and two foundations believing in us and in the obvious need offered a total of $70,000 over two years to fund these gatherings.

By nature we were not a group normally very patient about process. We were all very busy and productive in our various fields as pastors, authors, denominational officials, professors, lay consultants, and entrepreneurs. We wanted a fairly quick fix and we all had ideas of what was needed based on our own expertise, research data, and personal experience; but we stayed the course. We read books, we accepted research assignments, we instructed one another, and we met with other experts in various parts of the country as we tried to listen, learn, and propose alternatives.

Two of the initial group of eight had to drop out, and two others joined us, bringing their own special contributions. Month after month we met. As time passed we discovered that more than anything we were simply learning how much we loved and valued one another and our time together, but we also kept focused on our target—designing a model of intervention for smaller congregations that could become a movement of God for their revitalization and joyful investment in doing the work of the kingdom.

We covenanted together to practice accountability each time we gathered, and employed a variation of what has become known as the L^3 Incubator model of leadership development (Loving, Learning, Leading), developed by one of our members, Craig Robertson. We spent time together in worship and prayer. We held one another accountable for reporting on how well we had done at being faithful to a discipline we had named the month before that would "help enhance [our] relationship with Jesus Christ and result in [our] becoming more Christlike and the leader God has in mind." We examined mounds of data related to the issues being faced by smaller churches and we dug into biblical and historical material looking for perspective. We constantly kept asking how what we were learning could create a true movement of lasting renewal and not just be another program or resource.

In time, and in fact at one specific meeting, we almost felt overwhelmed with something that happened. All of the pieces came together around the image of "abiding" from John 15. The answer had to involve a lively and intimate relationship with Christ, a deep appreciation of one another, accountable discipleship, a priority focus on being fruitful, and a joyful delight in glorifying God. As we sought to combine all of the lessons gleaned through fifteen months of work and prayer, the best word to describe the new offering we wanted to make was simply *abide*.

Our goal was to aid in the development of an ongoing discipleship-leadership team for each congregation that would participate. We came to believe that ongoing renewal, turnaround and beyond, begins with a deep sense of personal and conceptual renewal that is nurtured in groups holding each member accountable in love. The end, however, is not just for personal transformation but also for a movement of God's mission in the world—for fruit, much fruit, "fruit that will last" (John 15:16). We were aware of the problem created by pastoral leadership transitions in smaller churches, and experienced a similar sense of loss as we went through changes in the makeup of our own group. However, we quickly recovered because we had become a true leadership team that owned our calling and our L^3 process of Loving, Learning, and Leading together.

It dawned on us that what we were designing was not new. In fact, it was rather ancient but had been recovered again and again to enable true renewal movements to take wing and keep flying. Most of us also recognized it as a recapitulation of the early Wesleyan revival. John and Charles Wesley discerned that unless Christian disciples were bound together in special groups, the momentum of both their personal growth and that of the movement would fail. These brothers required every new member of the movement to be in a small accountability group known simply as a class meeting. Week after week persons had to respond to their class leader's inquiry of how it was with their souls and rehearse the degree to which they had succeeded or failed in their pursuit of God and godly living. This was expected of both those who already knew what grace meant through fully trusting in Christ alone for their salvation, and for those still trying to discern and experience this reality. As long as persons continued in the movement they had to continue to meet weekly in class or move to another level of disciplined life in groups designed for aiding their progression in holiness and service. Sadly, this model of accountable discipleship and leadership development was abandoned by Methodists in North America during the nineteenth century, a decision undoubtedly contributing to their decline during the twentieth century.

The two other groups instituted by the Wesleys proved to be most helpful in our reflection: (1) the bands, which continued the disciplines of the class meeting but with greater focus on overcoming sin and the pursuit of holiness, and (2) the select band (or select society), formed mostly to enhance a deep love for God and one another through trust and mutual sharing and to create a leadership team for each society (what we might today call a congregation) and for the entire movement. In this group, there was no designated leader, but all were fully engaged in speaking freely and discerning God's guidance for the whole endeavor.

We had stumbled on the benefits of all three groups wrapped up in one. What would happen, we asked, if teams combining the benefits of the class, the band, and the select band could be launched in thousands of smaller churches? Could this threefold "Wesleyan" approach of committing to accountable discipleship, developing a bond of love, and learning how to lead together— our L^3 ABIDE model—help produce a renewal movement that could both assist in initial turnaround and survive the beyond of pastoral transitions because the leadership and ownership of the vision would remain intact? We had confidence that it could and officially launched the Small Church Leadership Initiative (SCLI)[2] and the ABIDE project to assist in the development of such teams.

One New Contribution toward a Renewing Movement

Many millions of dollars are being invested these days by foundations, denominational organizations, and educational institutions to study and provide resources for a multitude of struggling smaller congregations. Most of the funding and creative energy toward the goal of revitalization and turnaround in these churches is aimed at shaping the lives of the pastors who serve them. More and more it is being realized that these do not have to be fully seminary-trained pastors, but they do need to understand their unique contribution as a leader within the context and culture of smaller congregations. This book is in part an effort to clarify some of the gifts, skills, and strategies such pastors need to utilize in order to be successful at their calling. But it is also now clear that the larger solution involves more than identifying and educating pastors. A true renewal movement for thousands of smaller congregations needs to embed into the life of each fellowship of disciples a DNA that is owned by a core group of leaders who protect it and pass it on. This is the unique design of ABIDE.

ABIDE begins with decisions made by a group of at least ten congregations (and judicatory leaders) agreeing to host the project. The goal is to have at least five persons from each church, including the pastor, commit to participate in the initial overnight retreat that is usually held on a Friday night and Saturday. After helpful introductions, orientation, and some time of getting acquainted, those gathered sing their faith together and share in a time of worship.

The teaching focus of the first evening is an introduction to the overarching purpose of ABIDE: "Churches Abiding in Christ, Advancing God's Mission, and Alive in God's Glory." The John 15 passage is examined with an emphasis on abiding in Christ and the priority of love. Table groups discuss the meaning of this image for themselves and for their congregations, and the evening concludes with another time of worship and prayer.

Saturday begins with breakfast together followed by another time of worship. One of the early themes for day two is an introduction to the ABIDE L^3 model of Loving, Learning, Leading. The teaching and discussion are punctuated with stories and testimonies of the impact of this approach on Christian development. A second theme focuses on the meaning of the glory of God to begin equipping persons with new eyes to see God at work around them, within them, and in their congregations. Stories are recounted of congregations moving from a sense of being inglorious to recapturing a sense of participating in

God's glory as those "created for my glory" (Isaiah 43:7). Table discussion focuses on "glory sightings"—places and moments when the glorious activity of God was observed in our daily lives and in the life of our congregations.

The remainder of the day includes examining a layperson's journey into discipleship and congregational team leadership, the importance of having a dream or vision for God's best, the centrality of prayer, God's mission for us in the world, and a brief introduction to the L³ ABIDE process. Closing worship and Communion conclude the first event. Each team's members determine before leaving if they wish to continue in the process, be faithful to weekly team meetings and assignments contained in the ABIDE notebook, and return in a month for a one-day Saturday retreat equipping them to move on to the next phase.

The second one-day retreat reviews and reinforces the earlier emphases and the team members experience emerging out of the weekly assignments. We begin again with worship followed by a time of sharing glory sightings. In the simplest terms, this is an inspiring session of hearing about answers to prayer, deep appreciation for their team, new insights for faithful discipleship, and recognition of God's special interventions. It's a new-fashioned time of testimony and witness to the abiding presence of Christ in the power of the Holy Spirit to the glory of the Father.

The teaching sessions examine biblical themes related to smallness, the overarching promises of God declaring, "I am with you," and a return to the message of John 15. With a bit more reflection on our mission as the body of Christ and appropriate breaks and table discussion, the rest of the day introduces in more detail the full L³ process and its significance for bringing about personal, congregational, as well as community transformation. This includes introducing the main themes explored in the months to come as the teams continue to grow in love, in knowledge, and in confidence as spiritual and missional leaders in their congregation.

The afternoon ends with a general question-and-answer time, a description of the ongoing coaching process provided by ABIDE, and an opportunity for each congregation to continue its covenant and participate in the year-long L³ process. New assignments are given and the date and location are announced for the next meeting of the teams with their ABIDE coaches. Worship concludes the day with a moving reminder of Christ's promise, "I am with you always."

As a movement ABIDE is still young, flexible, and developing. Only God knows how it will ultimately contribute to both turnaround and beyond. But these illustrative comments by two pastors and a layperson in the program offer a great sense of hope:

> The ABIDE program has become a foundational piece of our ministry and provided great opportunity in two venues of growth within our small rural churches. A growth in spirituality through a deepening personal relationship with Jesus Christ has been experienced by each ABIDE team member and they are sharing that growth with the congregation virtually on a daily basis. *And* a growth in membership and attendance numbers has occurred as a direct correlation to the information and tools provided by the ABIDE program. ABIDE truly enables and empowers churches to achieve the goal that was set on the first day the program was introduced to me. . . . Churches ABIDING in Christ, ADVANCING God's mission, and ALIVE in God's glory.
>
> Reverend Gregg, Pastor, North Carolina

The Gamewell team sings the praises of ABIDE at any chance they have. If we accomplish no more than what we have already experienced, I call the time a success and I look forward to watching God work through this team in the future.

Prior to enrolling in ABIDE our church thought it had lost its luster. ABIDE taught us that the luster was still there and began to help us learn how to rub that luster to a sheen and experience God's glory for the small church. ABIDE has brought our team members closer to God and closer to each other. In only six months we have seen the excitement from the ABIDE team spill over into our worship and other ministries.

Spirituality has made ALL the difference in the ABIDE experience. A key component in ABIDE is spiritual leadership through spiritual disciplines and accountability, which is either missing or less significant in many church revitalization programs. As a pastor, it is thrilling to watch church members begin to grow in their personal walk, metamorphosing into a spiritually led leader within the church & community. ABIDE understands that God wants glory for all churches, regardless of size, and that the Holy Spirit is excitingly active "wherever two or more are gathered" in Christ's name. In fact, you just might hear one of your members cry out "GLORY!" as they tell you what God is doing in their lives and in the life of the church!

Reverend Renee, Pastor, North Carolina

Not only are we in our Abide Group becoming better disciples and striving to live within the will of God, but we are starting to have a vision for our church and community, one that will bring glory to God and reach and teach the lost sheep. Before our Abide group began, many of us were disconnected from God and did not have a unified direction. Now we do. It is an exciting time within our team! Our church has already started to show a positive response to our Abide team and its sense of direction in the seven months we have been together.

Josh, Layperson, Texas

Pruning and Promises

In keeping with the image of "the vine and the branches" from John 15 the ultimate shaping of both our individual lives and expressions of Christ's church must be in the hands of the skilled Gardener, Jesus' Father (vv. 1-2). Jesus describes this as "pruning," something that few of us would normally volunteer for. Cutting away part of our lives for the sake of greater fruitfulness sounds not only sacrificial but also painful. Yet such pruning is related to the purpose the vinegrower has for the vine and thus for its branches.

One time when I was speaking about the John 15 image in Oklahoma, a man shared a profound lesson he had learned as a young boy growing up on a farm. One spring his father took him behind the barn to observe a grape arbor with just one vine. He asked his son to take note that the new growth was coming along just fine, but that this year he would do nothing to prune it. As the grapes came into their own for harvest, my new friend informed me that the vine produced only about thirty smaller bunches of grapes to pick and enjoy. The next spring his father took him back to the arbor and reminded him of the results of the previous year. Then he told him to note the difference good pruning would make this second year. The result—over 300 fat bunches of luscious grapes that year! I told him I had no idea of the significance of pruning. I confessed that one year I had quite unintentionally pruned three young grape vines I had planted along my fence with my lawnmower. He laughed and reminded me his father knew what he was doing.

I am not skilled at pruning even my own life, never mind someone else's. Proper trimming of our spiritual lives for the sake of more fruit is best left in the hands of our Father who knows us and knows our congregations. This is why prayer is so important. Discerning what God wants to communicate to us toward this end should be pursued patiently, prayerfully, and carefully together. Ultimately, pruning is about focusing our otherwise undisciplined lives toward a greater end, and it is not to be undertaken by "amateurs" with lawnmowers, whether clergy or lay.

It is fascinating in this passage how this act of fairly radical shaping is about enriching the flow and fruit of the love of God, not only for our own good but also for the good of others. The writer of Hebrews makes a similar observation.

> Endure trials for the sake of discipline. God is treating you as children; for what child is there whom a parent does not discipline? If you do not have that discipline in which all children share, then you are illegitimate and not his children. Moreover, we had human parents to discipline us, and we respected them. Should we not be even more willing to be subject to the Father of spirits and live? For they disciplined us for a short time as seemed best to them, but he disciplines us for our good, in order that we may share his holiness. Now, discipline always seems painful rather than pleasant at the time, but later it yields the peaceful fruit of righteousness to those who have been trained by it. (Hebrews 12:7-11)

Pruning is about discipline, shaping us for holiness and righteousness both as individuals and as fruitful congregations for the sake of our communities and, in fact, the entire world.

When we realize that the purpose of the Father and the Son in the power of the Spirit is only accomplished as we allow this pruning, we will pray: "Dear God, what is it you wish to remove and reshape in our lives that we might be more fruitful?" Although the many ideas examined in this study of turnaround churches might be very helpful in discerning the pruning God intends in your congregation, be careful not to settle for a strategy and ignore the Spirit's guidance. That's a little like pruning with a lawnmower. I can assure you, it's not a good approach.

One Final Look at Abiding

In the words of Jesus:

> "I am the true vine, and my Father is the vinegrower. He removes every branch in me that bears no fruit. Every branch that bears fruit he prunes to make it bear more fruit. You have already been cleansed by the word that I have spoken to you. Abide in me as I abide in you. Just as the branch cannot bear fruit by itself unless it abides in the vine, neither can you unless you abide in me. I am the vine, you are the branches. Those who abide in me and I in them bear much fruit, because apart from me you can do nothing. Whoever does not abide in me is thrown away like a branch and withers; such branches are gathered, thrown into the fire, and burned. If you abide in me, and my words abide in you, ask for whatever you wish, and it will be done for you. My Father is glorified by this, that you bear much fruit and become my disciples. As the Father has loved me, so I have loved you; abide in my love. If you keep my commandments, you will abide in my love, just as I have kept my Father's commandments and abide in his love. I have said these things to you so that my joy may be in you, and that your joy may be complete.
>
> "This is my commandment, that you love one another as I have loved you. No one has greater love than this, to lay down one's life for one's friends. You are my friends if you do what I command you. I do not call you servants any longer, because the servant does not know what the master is doing; but I have called you friends, because I have made to you everything that I have heard from my Father. You did not choose me but I chose you. And I appointed you to go and bear fruit, fruit that will last, so that the Father will give you whatever you ask him in my name. I am giving you these commands so that you may love one another." (John 15:1-17)

I conclude with a few thoughts on the promises of God in these verses. It's not just the pruning that captures our attention. Take a look at the promises mentioned when this abiding becomes our whole life.

First, the promise is that every branch that bears no fruit will be cut off and every branch that bears some fruit will be pruned to bear more fruit (15:2).

Second, we are promised that if we abide in him and his word abides in us, we can ask for anything we need and it will be given to us (15:7).

Third, we are promised that if we truly abide in Jesus we will bear much fruit, prove that we really are becoming his disciples, and bring glory to God (15:8).

Fourth, comes that wonderful word reminding us that if we keep these commandments, we will know the ongoing blessing of divine love, the medicine of life (15:10, 17).

Fifth, all of this is to give to us the quite amazing gift of living in heavenly joy and being called friends, not just servants, by our Lord (15:11, 15).

These are *beyond* all that we could ask or think. What more can be said that would not be a distraction rather than an addition? Perhaps only these words that come as a song that can wash over our souls and remind us of who we are, whose we are, and why we are God's people, disciples of Jesus, fruitful branches bearing the fruit of eternal Love.

> Love divine, all loves excelling,
> joy of heaven, to earth come down;
> Fix in us thy humble dwelling;
> all thy faithful mercies crown!
> Jesus thou art all compassion,
> pure, unbounded love thou art;
> Visit us with thy salvation;
> enter every trembling heart.
> Breathe, O breathe thy loving Spirit
> into every troubled breast!
> Let us all in thee inherit;
> let us find that second rest.
> Take away our bent to sinning;

Alpha and Omega be;
End of faith, as its beginning,
  set our hearts at liberty.
Come, Almighty to deliver,
  let us all thy life receive;
Suddenly return and never,
  nevermore thy temples leave.
Thee we would be always blessing,
  serve thee as thy hosts above,
Pray and praise thee without ceasing,
  glory in thy perfect love.
Finish, then, thy new creation;
  pure and spotless let us be.
Let us see thy great salvation
  perfectly restored in thee;
Changed from glory into glory,
  till in heaven we take our place,
Till we cast our crown before thee,
  lost in wonder, love, and praise.[3]

Questions for Discussion

• What are the most significant lessons for your personal life that emerge from the John 15 passage?

• Jesus describes in John 15 five dynamics related to bearing much fruit: (1) being cleaned or cut back for a new growing season, (2) abiding in him and having his word abide in us, (3) being pruned to take away extraneous and life-draining activities, (4) loving with the love that comes from God, and (5) living joyfully in obedience to his teachings. Which of these seems most needed today for your congregation to become more fruitful for God's glory?

- The ABIDE model emphasizes a group process known as L³ (Loving, Learning, and Leading) for developing a strong leadership team. When have you been part of a team that experienced something like this?

- Where is something like this L³ model currently at work in developing leadership for your church?

- Considering all you have read in this book, what three lessons could prove most helpful in leading your congregation to turnaround and beyond?

APPENDIX
Participating Pastors and Contributors

Calvin Aardsma
Thomas W. Albert
Paul Anderson
Anthony Louis Antonelli
David W. Baldridge
Stanley Barkdoll
Ray Barkey
Billy J. Bass
Patty L. Beagle
Bobby Bell
David Bell
Eric A. D. Bell
Timothy R. Boeglin
Jeannine Brenner
David Bromstad
David Brown
Mark Buchanan
R. David Chambers
Robert L. Chapman
Michael D. Cloyd
Bob Coleman
Creg Crispell
John Culbertson
Larry M. Dentler
Joseph F. DiPaolo
James Steven Drury
Ronald Dull
Michael Duncan
Jeff Dunn

Don Duvall
Bob Edwards
Missy Elliott
Kendal Elmore
Eugene L. Feagin
Barbara Florey
Larry A. Frank
Steve Garnaas-Holmes
Sylvester Gillespie
John Goering
J. R. Gonzales
Don Graham
Dennis Hamshire
J. Val Hastings Jr.
William N. Hay Sr.
Richard Hayward
David Herndon
Leonard Higgins
Thomas D. Hindman
John Homer
Lou Hornberger
Dale Hylton
Darrin Lee Jones
Donald Jones
William R. Keeffe
Bill Kemp
Ed Kerr
Tom Kraft
John Kuritz

Duane A. Lewellen
Chris Livermore
Gil Livingston
William Longenecker
Sherrin Marshall
O. Phillip May
Kipp McClury
S. Renee McKenzie
Art McPhee
Danny McVey
Douglas Milliron
Richard D. Moore
Kirk W. Morledge
Paul C. Murphy
Mary Jane Myer
Marcelle G. Myers
Hal Noble
Willis E. Osban
J. Fred Parklyn
Gregg Parris
Norman W. Parsons
Sharon Patch
Richard A. Paul
Linda M. Peabody
Donald E. Peters Jr.
Herb Phar
Hazel J. Porter
Steven J. Porter
Linda Poteete-Marshall
W. Ford Price
Yolanda Pupo-Ortiz
Alan Rice
L. V. Rigney
C. Martin Riley

Dennis O. Rinehart
Craig Robertson
Eduardo Roque
Edward Rosenberry
R. Branson Sheets III
Gerald Shoap
Richard Shover
Ruth Lantz Simmons
Bryan E. Siverly
Patricia A. Small
Lee Smedley
John Southwick
Dennis Spangler
Billy D. Strayhorn
Jim Sullivan
Lowell H. Swisher
Wee-Li Tan
James Thomas
Richard F. Thornton
Neal and Kathie Timpson
James A. Vander Slik
Tom Vencuss
Bob Vickerys
J. Peter Vosteen
Grace C. Washington
Duane W. Waters
Earl F. Watterson
Russell West
Roger P. Windell
Norma Wingo
Charles and Linda Yarborough
Richard Zamostny
Maximilian Zurdt

Notes

1. Pathways to Turnaround

1. John Wesley, "Thoughts upon Methodism," in *The Works of John Wesley: The Methodist Societies History, Nature, and Design*, vol. 9, ed. Rupert Davies (Nashville: Abingdon, 1989), 527.

2. Thomas J. Peters and Robert H. Waterman, *In Search of Excellence: Lessons from America's Best-Run Companies* (New York: HarperBusiness, 2004), 119, 156, 200, 235, 279, 292, 306.

3. Robert H. Waterman Jr., *The Renewal Factor: How the Best Get and Keep the Competitive Edge* (New York: Bantam, 1987).

4. Jim Collins, *Good to Great* (New York: HarperCollins, 2001), 11.

5. Ibid., 12–13.

6. Ken Blanchard and Phil Hodges, *Lead Like Jesus: Lessons from the Greatest Leadership Role Model of All Time* (Nashville: W Publishing Group, 2005), 79.

7. Howard A. Snyder, *Signs of the Spirit: How God Reshapes the Church* (Grand Rapids, Mich.: Academie Books, 1989), 11. Howard Snyder is now retired from his teaching position at Asbury Theological Seminary but still gives leadership, together with other interested colleagues, to The Center for the Study of World Christian Revitalization Movements and edits its bulletin.

8. Ibid., 32.

9. Ibid., 276.

10. Ibid., 300.

11. Ibid., 300–310.

12. Ibid., 301, 302, 303, 304, 305, 306, 307, 308, 309, 310.

13. Rose Sims, *The Dream Lives On* (Wilmore, Ky.: Bristol, 1989), 11.

14. Ibid.

15. Ibid., 69.

16. Seven questions proved to be very helpful in clarifying these turnaround strategies, namely: (1) What three primary factors do you think most impede smaller churches from becoming revitalized and engaged in effective ministry and evangelism? (2) What obstacles have you faced in leading this church to new life and growth? (3) What efforts were made to overcome these obstacles? (4) What three primary factors do you think most enable smaller churches to become revitalized and engaged in effective ministry and evangelism? (5) What factors have contributed most to the growth of this congregation over the last few years? (6) What intentional efforts were made to contact, welcome, evangelize, and assimilate unchurched people into your congregation? (7) What stages, steps, or turning points were most obvious to you as this church went through its transition to new life and growth?

2. Pastors as Turnaround Leaders

1. Carl Dudley, *New Possibilities for Small Churches,* ed. Douglas Alan Walwrath (New York: Pilgrim, 1983), 46.

2. See the results of Warren Hartman's 1980 survey of 330 pastors of smaller United Methodist churches in *There's New Life in the Small Congregation* by Ronald K. Crandall and L. Ray Sells (Nashville: Discipleship Resources, 1983), 35. Hartman's survey showed growing smaller churches were less likely than stable and declining churches to be pastored by full seminary graduates.

3. Drawing on Ferdinand Tonnie's distinction between *gemeinschaft* and *gesellschaft* (*Community and Society,* 1887), and Robert Redfield's distinctions between "Folk Society" and "Urban Society," Anthony Pappas offers an interesting analysis of the small church as "tribe" in his book *Money, Motivation, and Mission in the Small Church* (Valley Forge, Pa.: Judson, 1989), chapters 3 and 4. Lyle Schaller explored the same idea earlier in his chapter "Tribes, Movements, and Organizations" in *Getting Things Done* (Nashville: Abingdon, 1987).

4. Carl Dudley certainly draws on this image in *Effective Small Churches in the Twenty-first Century* (Nashville: Abingdon, 2003). Perhaps

this is best seen by his very helpful image that growth in membership is primarily by "adoption."

5. Warren Bennis and Burt Nanus, *Leaders: The Strategies for Taking Charge* (New York: Harper & Row, 1985), 21.

6. Mortimer Arias traces this theme in his book *Announcing the Reign of God* (Philadelphia: Fortress, 1984). The one significant exception he notes to the loss of this theme is E. Stanley Jones who "gladly acknowledged he was 'obsessed' with the Kingdom of God, and who consistently tried for half a century to present the gospel in that perspective, relating it to the quest of modern man and the problems of society" (123).

7. Howard Snyder addresses this concern in several of his books and, as was noted in chapter 1, he includes it as the overarching theme and vision needed for building a renewal strategy for the local church. It is interesting to note that while the image of the kingdom of God has sometimes been viewed as a theme mostly of interest to "social activists," the World Evangelical Fellowship's publication of David Kornfield's work *Church Renewal: A Handbook for Christian Leaders* (Exeter: Paternoster; Grand Rapids, Mich.: Baker, 1989) begins: "What brings renewal in our lives? There are two dimensions—the *dream* and the *journey*. The dream comes from God. As we tune our hearts to his, our vision of his desires becomes clearer. The journey is living out the dream—putting into practice the vision God gives us. This manual is meant to help clarify our vision, . . . a vision for the Kingdom of God. This vision provides the framework for everything God intends his Church to be" (3–5).

8. R. Robert Cueni, *What Ministers Can't Learn in Seminary: A Survival Manual for the Parish Ministry* (Nashville: Abingdon, 1988), 127–28.

9. James E. Cushman, *Beyond Survival: Revitalizing the Small Church* (Parsons, W.Va.: McClain Printing, 1981), 91–92.

3. Turning toward the Spirit

1. These trends and others affecting small rural churches were documented in a report of rural churches in Missouri thirty years ago by Edward W. Hassinger, John S. Holki, and J. Kenneth Benson in *The Rural Church: Learning from Three Decades of Change* (Nashville: Abingdon, 1988).

2. Clark Morphew, "Survey: Methodists Want Docile Clergy," *The [Akron] Beacon Journal,* July 31, 1993, A9–A10.

3. Howard Snyder, *Signs of the Spirit: How God Reshapes the Church* (Grand Rapids, Mich.: Academie Books, 1989), 285–91.

4. The Presbyterian Survey, July/August 1992, 9. Additional information on this program and a 52-page manual are available by writing the church at 2130 Ulric St., San Diego, CA 92111 or calling (619) 277–0523.

5. Martha Grace Reese, *Unbinding the Gospel: Real Life Evangelism* (St. Louis: Chalice Press, 2006), 42.

6. For additional information on this ecumenical and international model for spiritual renewal and the development of Christian leaders, write *The Walk to Emmaus,* The Upper Room, 1908 Grand Avenue, P.O. Box 189, Nashville, TN 37202, or phone (615) 340–7200. Tens of thousands of new "pilgrims" (persons who attend the retreat weekend) and their congregations are refreshed by this program every year.

7. Leander E. Keck, *The Church Confident* (Nashville: Abingdon, 1993), 25.

8. Ibid., 39.

9. William H. Willimon and Robert L. Wilson, *Preaching and Worship in the Small Church,* Creative Leadership Series, ed. Lyle E. Schaller (Nashville: Abingdon, 1980).

10. Laurence A. Wagley, *Preaching with the Small Congregation* (Nashville: Abingdon, 1989).

11. David Ray, *Wonderful Worship in Smaller Churches* (Cleveland: Pilgrim, 2000); Robin Knowles Wallace and Terry R. Heck, *Worship in Small Membership Churches* (Nashville: Discipleship Resources, 2007).

12. David L. Lattimer, "Becoming a Christian in the Churches of Christ in Christian Union" (D.Miss. diss., Asbury Theological Seminary, 1991), 125.

13. The most significant reminders of the importance of small groups came from the comments of members interviewed and from the pastors' answers to questions about new members and programs for Christian maturation.

14. James E. Cushman, *Beyond Survival: Revitalizing the Small Church* (Parsons, W.Va.: McClain Printing, 1981), 20.

15. Ibid., 123, 124.

16. David Stark, Patrick Keifert, Judy Stack-Nelson, *The Small Church Small Group Guide* (St. Paul: Church Innovations, 1998), 20–27.

4. Overcoming the Obstacles

1. Joseph F. DiPaolo, *You Shall Be My Witnesses: A History of Wissinoming United Methodist Church 1891–1991* (Acton, Mass.: Tapestry, 1992), 53, 54.

2. Lyle Schaller, *Growing Plans* (Nashville: Abingdon, 1983), 20.

3. Carl Dudley, "Events Worth Remembering," chap. 7 in *Effective*

Small Churches in the Twenty-first Century (Nashville: Abingdon, 2003), 118–32.

4. DiPaolo, *You Shall Be My Witnesses,* vii.

5. Harold Percy, *Your Church Can Thrive: Making the Connections That Build Healthy Congregations* (Toronto: ABC, 2003), 16–24.

6. David Heetland, "A Development Officer Looks at Stewardship," *Seminary Development News* (April 1993): 8–9.

7. Almost every recent book on ministry in smaller churches as well as other current texts on leadership offer at least one chapter on handling conflict. For example, see Nancy Folts, ed., *Religious Education in the Small Church* (Birmingham, Ala.: Religious Education, 1990), "Conflict, Feuds, and Border Wars" (chapter 9); and David Canada, *Spiritual Leadership in the Small Membership Church* (Nashville: Abingdon, 2005), "Roadblocks to the Journey" (chapter 4). Other writers tackle it head-on: Edward Dobson, Speed Leas, and Marshall Shelley, *Mastering Conflict and Controversy* (Portland, Ore.: Multnomah, 1992); Charles Cosgrove and Dennis Hatfield, *Church Conflict: The Hidden Systems Behind the Fights* (Nashville: Abingdon, 1994); and Peter L. Steinke, *Healthy Congregations: A Systems Approach* (Washington, D.C.: Alban Institute, 1996).

8. Norman Shawchuck and Robert Moeller, "Animal Instincts: Five Ways Church Members Will React in a Fight," *Leadership* (Winter 1993): 43–47.

9. Ibid., 44.

10. Ibid., 47.

11. Martin Luther, speaking before the Diet of Worms, April 18, 1521.

5. Turning toward Others

1. Doran McCarty, *Leading the Small Church* (Nashville: Broadman Press, 1991), 142.

2. For an excellent academic review of this problem through church history as it relates to the translation and meaning of evangelism, see David Barrett's *Evangelism! A Historical Survey of the Concept* (Birmingham: New Hope, 1986). Barrett acknowledges that in spite of the fact that "to evangelize" primarily means to tell the gospel, the task must not be separated from all that Jesus said and did to make the gospel of the kingdom clear and visible. He also offers several biblical words and images besides "to preach the gospel" to clarify the meaning of evangelism and to bring it more in line with the larger task of the great commission, which is to make disciples.

3. The Mainline Evangelism Project summarized by Martha Grace Reese in *Unbinding the Gospel* (St. Louis: Chalice, 2006) examined 30,000

congregations in six denominations, looking for churches that had reached new adults with the gospel. They found one-half of 1 percent (.005), or 150 churches, that had baptized 5 adults each year for three consecutive years. Reese writes: "The median age of our high baptism congregations was 96 years old. (Half of these congregations surveyed were had existed for more than 96 years.) It is now clear; a congregation may be too stuck in its ways to do evangelism, but it's not too old!" (31). Another bit of interesting research emerged in 2001, when George Barna released his statistics on the percentage of members in various denominations that had shared their faith with a non-Christian during the past year. Overall, mainline Protestants came in at 24 percent, while only the most rapidly growing Pentecostal and independent churches were above 60 percent. Two of the mainline denominations were as low as 10 and 14 percent, respectively (http://www.adherents.com/misc/activity.html).

4. See the breakdown of these percentages in chapter 2 under the heading "Personal Backgrounds." If winning others because it is "natural" as our new nature, and because we desire to see them changed can be called "pull" motivation, 76.8 percent of the pastors indicated they work at evangelism from this source of energy. If obedience to Christ's commands can be called "push" motivation, 22.1 percent of the pastors drew on this source for their motivation.

5. This Christian version of AA began in 1991 and has grown to be one of the most successful efforts incorporated by churches for helping persons caught in addictive behaviors. Information and guidelines for making use of the program can be found at its national website at http://www.celebraterecovery.com/.

6. Lyle Schaller, *Growing Plans* (Nashville: Abingdon, 1983), 9.

7. See two helpful resources I've written for equipping persons in Christian witness and evangelism: (1) *The Contagious Witness: Exploring Christian Conversion* (Nashville: Abingdon, 1995)—an examination of what can be learned from over 10,000 interviews reporting how persons came to faith in Christ; and (2) *Witness: Learning to Share Your Christian Faith* (Nashville: Discipleship Resources, 2007)—a twenty-five-week small-group pilgrimage on learning how to live daily as Christ's witnesses with greater effectiveness.

6. Developing True Disciples

1. Vision statement of the Episcopal Diocese of Western Massachusetts.

2. James M. Burns, *Leadership* (New York: Harper & Row, 1978).

3. R. Robert Cueni, *The Vital Church Leader* (Nashville: Abingdon, 1991), 17.

4. This is a summary of a description by B. M. Bass as cited in *Theories and Models in Applied Behavioral Science,* vol. 3, "Management/Leadership," ed. J. William Pfeiffer (San Diego: Pfeiffer and Company, 1991), 216.

5. James M. Kouzes and Barry Z. Posner, *The Leadership Challenge,* 4th ed. (San Francisco: Jossey-Bass, 2007).

6. George Barna, in his book *Revolution* (Carol Stream, Ill.: Tyndale House, 2005), writes: "I want to show you what our research has uncovered regarding a growing sub-nation of people, already well over 20 million strong, who are what we call Revolutionaries. . . . They have no use for churches that play religious games. . . . They are seeking a faith experience that is more robust and awe inspiring, a spiritual journey that prioritizes transformation at every turn, something worthy of the Creator whom their faith reflects" (13, 14). Barna describes these revolutionaries as being linked together for worship, spiritual growth, and significant ministry to others through smaller units or mini-networks of people who often participate in a house church or committed cell of Christians without the specific benefit of an "ordained" clergy leader. It almost sounds like a rediscovery of the movements Howard Snyder described earlier—like the earliest stages of the Methodist Revival. What if multitudes of smaller churches could serve this kind of function for people in the future instead of simply protecting a heritage and a tradition that no longer seem to be radical enough for serious Christian living?

7. Turnaround and Pastoral Transitions

1. Harvard Business Online, "Proven Strategies for Leadership Transition," http://harvardbusinessonline.hbsp.harvard.edu/.

2. Denice Rothman Hinden and Paige Hull, "Executive Leadership Transition: What We Know," *The Nonprofit Quarterly* (Winter 2002): 20.

3. Ibid., 24.

4. *Executive Transitions Monograph Series,* vol. 1 (Baltimore: Annie E. Casey Foundation, 2004), 6–7.

5. *TransitionLeader:* The e-newsletter on nonprofit executive succession and transitions 2(1) (Summer 2004).

6. Ibid., 10.

7. Fourteen of the thirty-six churches able to be contacted and evaluated had lost momentum with the first transition of pastoral leadership and never regained it. One of these congregations reportedly was in a community experiencing significant population decline. Another ten

churches struggled through one or more pastoral transitions but reported they finally were regaining a sense of hope and renewal. Six still had the same pastoral leader and were excitingly healthy. One congregation with a pastoral transition suffered no loss of momentum, and another with a single transition gave evaluations that varied depending on which pastor reported.

8. *The Book of Discipline of The United Methodist Church* is reviewed and adjusted every four years in keeping with any changes passed by the General Conference gathering consisting of elected lay and clergy delegates from every Annual Conference (regional judicatory) of the denomination. In the 2004 edition, paragraphs 430 to 435 spell out the details of how appointments are made and describes a "consultative process," taking into account: (1) an annual review of the unique needs of the congregation involved, (2) an annual review of the gifts and graces of the pastors, and (3) a review of the community context as requested (added in 1996). More detailed descriptions of these procedures are spelled out in these paragraphs, and multiple efforts to create congregational resources for such reviews are continually being developed and published.

9. Similar lists can be found in several resources, but especially helpful is the checklist in Carolyn Weese and J. Russell Crabtree, *The Elephant in the Boardroom* (San Francisco: Jossey-Bass, 2004), 153–54.

10. Ibid., 6. Reprinted by permission.

11. Ibid., 13.

12. Some of the most helpful and least expensive approaches to evaluating readiness for leadership transitions are handbooks and workbooks designed for a small group of leaders. The Alban Institute offers several resources for pastoral transitions, including *Beginning Ministry Together: The Alban Handbook for Clergy Transitions* by Roy W. Oswald, Roy M. Oswald, James M. Heath, and Ann W. Heath (2003). A new eight-session resource specifically developed for United Methodists in western North Carolina by Nancy Burgin Rankin and Beverly Bowyer Coppley is *Checking Vital Signs: Assessing Your Local Church Potential* (Graham, N.C.: Plowpoint, 2007).

13. A growing number of United Methodist clergy are receiving training as interim ministers and committing themselves to this role. Bill Kemp, serving in the Western Pennsylvania Conference, is a part-time interim minister for smaller churches and an author. See his workbook especially designed for transitions in smaller churches: *The Church Transition Workbook: Getting Your Church in Gear* (Nashville: Discipleship Resources, 2004).

14. From the statement of purpose for SCLI (Small Church Leadership Initiative) and its ABIDE model for congregational renewal.

8. Turnaround and Beyond—Abiding

1. *The Works of John Wesley,* vol. 11, *The Appeals to Men of Reason and Religion and Certain Related Open Letters,* ed. Gerald R. Cragg (Nashville: Abingdon, 1992), 45.

2. SCLI is an LLC organization affiliated with a 501c-3 corporation known as Spiritual Leadership Inc. More information can be found at http://spiritual-leadership.org.

3. Charles Wesley, "Love Divine, All Loves Excelling," in *The United Methodist Hymnal* (Nashville: The United Methodist Publishing House), 384.

Subject Index

flexibility, 108
Francis, Saint, 25
Friendship Sundays, 94-95
fruitful, 38, 90, 99, 137, 148, 153, 158

gifts for ministry, 37, 44, 67, 85, 88, 105, 121-25
glory sightings, 156
goals, 25, 28, 70, 91-92, 117
God
    glory of, 2, 28, 74, 111, 155
    Holy Spirit, 2, 7, 13, 16, 20, 24, 27, 31, 34, 39, 40, 44, 51, 64, 126, 137, 141
    Holy Trinity, 148
gospel, 20, 25, 88, 94, 101, 104
grace, 6, 9, 26, 44, 51, 60, 61, 84, 116, 124
grasshopper mind-set, 54, 59
Great Commandment, 104
Great Commission, 24, 88, 127
Greenleaf, Robert, 6

Halverson, Richard, 147
Harvard Business Review, 131
Heck, Terry, 45
Heetland, David, 73
Hersey, Paul, 108
Hinden, Denice Rothman, 132
hope, 2, 10, 12, 20, 34, 40, 52, 64-65, 70, 102, 114-15, 133, 141, 145, 149, 157
Hull, Paige, 132
humor, 26, 114, 139

identity, 2, 8
incubator, 126
invitation, 62, 69-70, 84, 92-95

Jesus, 35, 148
    ministry of, 28, 62, 64, 69, 71, 88, 107-108, 137, 143, 148

joy, 149

Keck, Leander, 45
kingdom of God, 9, 24, 28, 72, 88, 98, 104, 137, 143
Kouzes, James, 111, 118

L^3 incubator model, 152, 156
Lattimer, David, 46
laypersons, 32, 85, 121-24
leadership
    authority, 15, 29
    Christian, 8
    exemplary, 111, 118
    for renewal, 5, 33
    functions, 9-12
    servant, 6
    situational, 108
    teams, 91, 133, 141, 145, 153, 156
    training, 44
    transactional, 109
    transformational, 109-10, 118, 127, 131
    transitions, 131-34, 140-41
learning, 16, 26, 40, 49, 51, 86, 91, 100-102, 111, 122, 126, 145, 152-55
listening, 27, 86, 93, 144
love, 16, 19, 25, 28, 35, 63, 95, 101, 104, 121, 149-51
Luther, Martin, 3, 25

Mainline Evangelism Study, 41
members (also membership), 11-13, 21, 92, 95, 101, 113, 119, 122, 136, 157
Methodists, 3, 7, 137, 154
mission, 8, 107-108, 112-18, 139-42, 144, 153, 156
mistakes, 25-28, 111
modeling, 111, 118
Moeller, Robert, 77

momentum, 20, 91, 106, 108, 123, 128, 131
Moravianism, 7
Morphew, Clark, 32
motivation, 18
music, 10

Nanus, Burt, 23
newcomers, 91, 96
The Nonprofit Quarterly, 132

obstacles, 55-60
outreach, 11, 25, 57, 68-71, 85, 96, 139
outsiders, 56, 68

Parris, Gregg, 39, 42-43
pastor, 11, 29, 36
   appointment of, 57, 132-33, 137-38, 141
   call of, 61, 64, 107, 110, 132-33, 137-38, 141
   incoming, 135, 138, 142-45
   interim, 58, 99, 141
   outgoing, 136-40
   second career, 50, 60, 70, 75, 110
   transitions, 13, 29, 33, 58, 129, 134-45
   tenure, 17, 36, 72
patience, 16, 20, 25-26, 57
Paul, the Apostle, 16, 25, 32, 88, 105, 120
Pentecost, 24
Percy, Harold, 66, 79
Peter, the Apostle, 25, 32, 62, 102
Peters, T. J., 4
Philip, the evangelist, 82
Phillips, J. B., 63, 79
pietism, 7
Posner, Barry, 111, 118
prayer, 12, 27, 38-42, 75, 84, 139, 141, 156, 159

preaching, 12, 19, 25, 45-47, 63, 114, 119
priorities, 67
programs, 85, 95-98, 117
prophets, 2
Protestant Reformation, 3
purpose, 65, 111, 115-18

questions, 64, 66, 69, 101-102, 115, 130

Ray, David, 45
Reese, Martha Grace, 41
renewal, 5, 7, 34
   dimensions, 34-35, 51
   movement, 152-55
risk, 12, 20, 25, 27, 36, 111
Robertson, Craig, 152
rural community, 33

Schaller, Lyle, 59, 98
SCLI, 154
self-image (esteem), 33, 59, 62, 74
seminary education, 18
Senge, Peter, 6
Shawchuck, Norman, 77
Sims, Rose, 11
sin, 26, 32, 124
small groups, 47-50, 125-26, 139, 144
Snyder, Howard, 7-9, 34-35
special events (and Sundays), 42-44, 62, 85, 88, 93
stewardship, 71-76, 139
strategic planning, 25, 64, 85, 112, 115-18
success, 4, 8, 18, 27, 63, 137, 157
Sunday school, 100, 114, 123
survival, 59, 77, 91, 130

teaching, 25, 91, 126
Tebbe, Don, 133
Tertullian, 148

training, 26, 91, 133, 137
transformation, 49, 104, 109-10, 127, 151
TransitionLeader, 133
turnaround, 1
churches, 9, 38, 96, 116, 129, 141, 143
leaders, 77, 110
pastors, 16-28, 107-28
stages, 75, 86, 109
strategies, 2, 12

vision, 2, 12, 20, 23-25, 55, 58, 63-68, 107, 110-11, 114-15, 139-40, 143-44
visitation, 10, 19, 25, 36, 61, 69, 70, 85, 98-102, 135
visitors, 86-88

Wagley, Laurence, 45
Walk to Emmaus, 43, 50
Wallace, Robin, 45
Waterman, R. H., 4
Watkins, Michael, 131
Weese, Carolyn, 140
welcome, 119-21, 127
Wesley, John, 3, 150, 153
Wesley, Susanna, 25
Wheatley, Margaret, 6
Willimon, Will, 45
Wilson, Bob, 45
witness, 81-82, 142
worship
    attendance, 92, 122, 157
    inspiring, 12, 45-47, 62, 85
    teams, 123

youth, 12, 84, 98

Scripture Index